AMERICAN RUSTIC

AMERICAN RUSTIC

Chase Reynolds Ewald

photographs by **Audrey Hall**

GIBBS SMITH
TO ENRICH AND INSPIRE HUMANKIND

For Charles —CRE

15 16 17 18 19   5 4 3 2

Text © 2015 by Chase Reynolds Ewald
Photographs © 2015 by Audrey Hall

Published by
Gibbs Smith
P.O. Box 667
Layton, Utah 84041

1.800.835.4993 orders
www.gibbs-smith.com

Designed by Sheryl Dickert
Printed and bound in Hong Kong

Gibbs Smith books are printed on either recycled, 100% post-consumer waste, FSC-certified papers or on paper produced from sustainable PEFC-certified forest/controlled wood source. Learn more at www.pefc.org.

Library of Congress Cataloging-in-Publication Data

Ewald, Chase Reynolds, 1963-
  American Rustic / Chase Ewald ; Photographs by Audrey Hall.
— First Edition.
    pages cm
  ISBN 978-1-4236-4027-1
1. Interior decoration—United States. 2. Decoration and ornament, Rustic—United States. I. Title.
  NK2002.E93 2015
747.0973—dc23

2015006310

Contents

Introduction

"Knock loudly & wait!"
The sign is hand painted on thick watercolor paper. Posted above a cast-bronze door knocker of a longhorn skull, its irregular edges stand out against a glossy coat of slightly chipped teal paint. This is the entrance to the studio of acclaimed painter William Matthews, and in its informality, playfulness and utter lack of pretension, the sign makes a decidedly original rustic statement.

American Rustic style, like Matthews' studio door, is relaxed, of the moment and highly individualistic. Its conviviality proffers a put-your-feet-up invitation. And as both a statement of place and a means of self-expression, a rustic built environment is always unique.

With its logs, twigs, burls and bark, American Rustic style is rooted in the Arts & Crafts movement, which in its time was a natural response to the rapid industrialization, homogenization and shift in populations from rural to urban areas in the nineteenth century. This sylvan style then, as today, spoke to a collective yearning for a simpler life and a return to nature's embrace amidst a noisy, increasingly crowded world. Passion for rustic style has waxed and waned over the decades, but it has never gone out of fashion. Like the log cabin itself, it is an iconic American expression that speaks to our history, our belief in the healing power of nature and our enduring desire to get away from it all.

American Rustic design found its highest expression in the last quarter of the nineteenth century in the expansive woodland fantasies that were the Great Camps of the Adirondacks and in monumental "parkitecture" epitomized by hotels like the Old Faithful Inn in Yellowstone and the Ahwahnee in Yosemite. But American rustic at its heart is not about grand statements. It's about human-scaled environments and appropriateness to the landscape, and it can be found in every region of the country, from seaside shacks in Maine to log lean-tos on Michigan's Upper Peninsula. It's expressed in adobe haciendas, Craftsman bungalows, West Coast houseboats and Alaskan trappers' cabins.

Characterized by humble materials and honest construction techniques, American Rustic design is timeless in its appeal. It is aspecific to any time period, yet it is always rooted in place. It goes beyond speaking of a region; it is a product of its immediate vicinity and its unique microclimate.

In recent years the style has evolved, but it remains as appealing as ever. The enduring attraction of cozy log cabins with cave-like interiors and heavy furnishings is tempered by a current desire for cleaner lines, good quality of light and, most of all, an original approach. *American Rustic* presents a fresh, contemporary take on rustic design. From rural compounds in upstate New York and Santa Fe casitas to mountain lodges along the spine of the Rockies and throughout the Greater Yellowstone, the projects in these pages represent a myriad of approaches from the genre's top designers. The resulting homes are as individual as their owners and designers, and they speak to the landscapes in which they are sited.

Today's American Rustic spans a wide spectrum, ranging from post-and-beam interiors furnished with Thomas Molesworth chairs and museum-quality Native American art to simple log cabins outfitted with repurposed items and funky flea market finds. At its most basic, American Rustic might be a writing-retreat-with-a-view made from a canvas wall tent filled with vintage collectibles; it can be taken down in a day and packed out on mules. Sitting just as lightly on the land but antipodal in its technology, an eco-conscious prefabricated home on an open plain in Idaho rests on a foundation of railroad ties so that it can be easily relocated. The idea, quite literally, is to leave no trace.

Filtered through the creative sensibility of the style's leading designers, the projects in these pages range from the whimsical to the intellectual, from the traditional to the bohemian, from the do-it-yourself to the contemporary. The homes showcased here present clean, modern-leaning design, original statements in furnishings and decor, and light, airy interiors. They run the gamut from lived-in and piled-on to clean and contemporary, where sleek lines combine with rugged elements and soft textures for unique modern-rustic interiors. Whatever the approach, each home is highly original and meticulously crafted, thoughtfully conceived, sensitively sited and beautifully executed. As is only appropriate with homes built in America's most stunning natural landscapes, each project considers sense of place its starting point. Rustic is the ultimate in place-based architecture.

The elements of Rustic remain much as they have always been. They're kid- and animal-friendly. They house books, art, handmade furniture, quirky collectibles, such as canoes, antlered items, and National Park memorabilia, vintage paintings by anonymous artists, and materials local to the area: wood, stone, bark, burls. Color is introduced through textiles, old signs, leather cushions, painted furniture and the occasional bold-hued wall, while live-edge tables or headboards or a balustrade made of branches add sculptural interest. The kitchen is a place where designers have to push themselves to balance modern needs and a desire for light with an appropriate heritage feel; they use oversized farmhouse sinks, graceful lighting, and reproduction ranges and refrigerators, often in eye-catching colors. Mudrooms offer an opportunity for whimsicality, while bedrooms demand luxurious fabrics and a cozy place to cocoon. Indoor-outdoor living spaces are essential and appear in all iterations, but it is the fireplaces that are central to rustic living. They ground the homes, generate literal and figurative warmth, create a refuge from the elements and provide a focal point. Thanks to a thriving craft in stonemasonry, talented architects make the most of them.

Despite technological innovations, touchstone materials have not changed over time. Leading designers working in the rustic genre continue to make ample use of reclaimed barnwood, stacked railroad timbers, exposed beams, repurposed iron and sheet metal and local stones. As Joe Roodell of Miller Architects points out, "The character that aged materials bring, you just can't make that with new materials." At the same time, they feel free to inject their own personalities and those of their clients into the projects. They layer textures, tone and patterns and employ one-of-a-kind objects. Designers introduce unusual repurposed items, such as a bench made from an ore cart, lighting fixtures fashioned from antique seltzer bottles or wallpaper constructed from reproduced and enlarged topographic maps.

In fine art, too, American Rustic has evolved. It has shifted away from classic representational western art and leans more toward abstract works, with lighter, more minimal framing, or classic black-and-white photography in gallery framing. Modern influences also appear in streamlined metal balustrades and elegant, sometimes ethereal, lighting fixtures—a far cry from ponderous wagon-wheel and antler assemblages of the John Wayne era. Today's rustic employs classic elements with architectural innovations and

surprises, like towers, bridges and unassuming entryways opening up to grand expanses. Living roofs and underground rooms mitigate mass and help structures blend into their surroundings.

Rustic style is inherently simple. But the seeming simplicity of many of today's new rustic homes belies their technical innovations, including passive solar and geothermal heating and myriad innovative, earth-friendly technologies. In fact, one of the most traditional-looking homes is actually the most contemporary in its exacting sustainable mission and ultimate LEED platinum certification. Rustic style is sustainably minded in other ways. Repurposing goes well beyond reclaimed woods and timbers to whole buildings, such as a calving shed turned into a rec room, or a caboose used as guesthouse. The repurposing of ranch items and tools is an endless source of inspiration and fun for many designers.

Building American Rustic is never an impersonal experience. Owners are hugely invested in projects, even when they work full-time in distant cities. A New York attorney who had dreamt of being an architect prioritized his schedule to accommodate weekly design meetings no matter where he was or what he had going on; he was involved in every single decision throughout the eighteen-month project. The owner of an Arts & Crafts bungalow turned her collecting into a major hobby, carefully curating a compendium of related items invested with meaning over a two-year period. An international businessman and art collector with multiple homes hired an architect, then did all his own interior design. A director-producer couple in Montana parlayed their production and editing experience into their home construction; while living on-site, they turned their search for unique materials into a full-blown mission, buying a trailer and crisscrossing the northern Rockies in search of treasures they could repurpose. They would return from scavenging trips with wood from barns slated for demolition, lichen-covered stone, sheets of corrugated steel, railroad-bridge timbers, a wagon wheel from a local saloon and old planks from rodeo bleachers, etched with graffiti wrought by teenage boys in the '50s.

Despite its adherence to tradition, American Rustic has evolved. Historically built by untrained woodsmen, off-season fishing guides, cowboys, and individual homesteaders using local materials and modest amounts of glass, today's rustic homes are designed by highly educated and seasoned professionals. Their structures are thoughtfully conceived, highly crafted, technologically advanced and filled with light. What hasn't changed is the primary mission of rustic elements. Their use results in homes that are grounded, that offer sanctuary, that have a sense of place, that are nature-based and appropriate to the landscape. In short, they belong.

Building with Intention

The homeowners knew they weren't in California anymore when they came home from a trip and found that an elk had attacked their house. Their first floor windows were shattered. Deep scratches were incised on the walls. Apparently, a large bull with an imposing set of antlers had mistaken his own reflection for a challenger. Their next surprise came during the call to their insurers. Yes, in fact, they were covered for wildlife damage. Not only that, in a new home made from recycled and repurposed materials on a historic ranch, the "elk patina," as the homeowners call it, merely added to its authenticity. Welcome to Montana!

The Los Angeles transplants were longtime outdoors and wildlife enthusiasts who had always loved the mountain West. Though they both enjoyed their work in the entertainment industry, they wanted to spend more time outdoors and in beautiful places. They had an epiphany around 1989, recalls the wife and designer/director of the project. "We were at the top of our game, but we felt there must be something more."

They looked to Montana, where their first home was large, custom-built and guest-filled—but only enjoyed as a weekend retreat. Over time they realized that they wanted to move to Montana permanently and become part of the community. They made a complete lifestyle change, with their primary goal being to live there full time. "The truth is, it took twenty years," says the wife.

Their second goal was to be part of the history of the region; this compelled them to buy a historic 300-acre ranch outside Livingston. The house came with two century-old log cabins, one of which they lived in for the first couple of years. "We toyed with the idea of staying there, updating and adding more light, but my husband had to bend over to go from room to room, the house wasn't fully insulated, wires were literally on the wall, the heating was with a wood stove, and you can't get rid of the mice." They also felt that since the original cabins were built on the edge of the property they weren't taking full advantage of the land.

Wise new westerners who take time to get to know their land, walking it seasonally and daily, are spared the long-term consequences of enthusiastic but hasty decisions. Ultimately the pair identified three sites for a new home. One was located on a bend in the creek—a gorgeous spot, but it had the potential to flood and would have necessitated cutting a lot of trees. Another was on an upper bench, a working hay field. The site had 360-degree views and looked out at four mountain ranges. But Paradise Valley is known for its wind, and the site was deemed too exposed.

Ultimately they selected a natural clearing identified on topographic maps as the Little Meadow. It's an open oval surrounded by trees. "We have no wind here, we don't get the flooding, and we don't have to worry about cottonwood trees falling down. Also, in the meadow there's lots of wildlife seeking refuge from development in the valley—bears, mountain lions, wolves, deer, and beaver. It's like a mini Yellowstone Park."

The next step was to choose an architect. The couple knew they wanted their home to have sense of place and gesture to history. At the same time, they wanted a home comfortable enough for year-round living. In grappling with the question of how to design for both, they came across the work of Candace Miller.

Although Miller's office is just a short drive away, the wife recalls, they had never met. "I wanted to design a house but I needed help because I'm not an architect. I started looking through books and every house I loved had been designed by Candace Miller. We met and became instant friends. I was very involved, probably more than she's used to," she laughs.

She was involved because the couple, a professional producer and director, knew exactly what they wanted. "I wanted a house that was going to embrace me. Winter is long here. Everyone says summer lasts three months and winter lasts nine months. In summer, you're outdoors all the time; in winter, you're indoors. Coming from California we were used to light. Here we have true divided light windows running from floor to ceiling. It was a big concession for us because we have a lot of art, but we opted for windows over art."

It was a perfect job for the Livingston-based architect, who loves ranch architecture. "We worked closely with these homeowners on everything," Miller says. "They had lived on their land in a log cabin, a round-log building with peeled logs; it was very bright and yellow. She said she'd like something with patina. We went to view a couple of projects and started figuring out her desired palette. They wanted to bring in things they had found on their travels. She had lived in France, so blues and yellows were important. She was very sensitive to creating intimate spaces."

The clients had begun collecting materials and interesting items long before construction began, from reclaimed timbers and galvanized steel to found pieces from their ranch. Soon they were looking at whole buildings from which to construct their home, as well as lichen-bedecked rocks—found, not quarried—from Harlowton, Montana.

"I wanted rustic-French-farmhouse-meets-western-with-modern-aesthetic," explains the wife, "and I wanted to incorporate all parts of our lives." They were able to do that by using beams and natural plaster in French provincial tones. They were also strongly influenced by "parkitecture"; they looked at lots of buildings with big stone bases for reference, and to decide on appropriate scale.

The resulting home takes as its starting point two vintage hand-hewn cabins; one forms the living room, one the guest suite. Additional rooms and hallways—a bright airy kitchen with unique creative features, a cozy TV room—join them together. These are made from historic square log buildings purchased for the project. Says the owner, "They'd take them apart log by log, number them and put them back together like a jigsaw puzzle. They'd get sawn in half lengthwise then use traditional framing. There's a layer in between which makes the house airtight."

All the timbers in the home come from a friend's barn, which in turn had been constructed from old railroad bridge timbers that had been floated down the Yellowstone River. Every piece of wood in the house—the floors, stairs, molding, window trim—is recycled, with one exception: the walnut butcher block island. Almost every ceiling is different, too. The couple heard the old rodeo seating in Ennis, Montana, was being torn out; they procured the wood, and now one ceiling is made of rodeo benches. They bought a derelict barn that was completely unusable except for the galvanized steel of the roof. They left some of it natural and rolled some of it and used it in different ways.

"There are stories for everything," says the wife. "The huge sink in the utility room came from a friend's place in eastern Montana. It weighed about 500 pounds, and has giant porcelain legs. We needed half the community to get it onto the truck. It's beautiful and I use it constantly. In Montana you have to wash off your boots all the time."

They tried hard to incorporate things they found on the ranch, and used a lot of found and repurposed antiques. An old metal sanding table, now occupying pride of place in the front hall, for instance, was found lying on its side in a field. The couple worked directly with artisans as well on such projects as welded rods for the stairwell. "This is a house about materials more than anything else. It's truly a handcrafted house. It doesn't have the high drama of our house in Malibu. It's really about embracing, which you need here. It's November and it's 5 degrees out. It was minus 15 the other night. It's probably going to be like this until May. So you really need a warm environment."

In this they have succeeded. Built with intention and meaning, the house does appear part of the landscape and part of its history. Comfortably weathered, it is sturdy enough to withstand long Montana winters—and even the occasional elk attack.

Reclaimed materials and large expanses of glass characterize a home that's at one with its environment. The owners take advantage of the outdoor dining area all summer, while a balcony off the master bedroom is the perfect platform for wild-life viewing and afternoon naps.

The library, designed to be small and cozy, is furnished with antiques (a barrel from Maine, an old pine chest from Montana) and lined with bookshelves made of reclaimed wood. A Robert Bateman painting hangs under ceilings made of galvanized tin recycled from barns.

FACING: The living room, made from a reclaimed cabin and anchored by its fireplace made of Harlowton stone, is furnished with antiques and a Jerry Iverson oil painting. The chandelier comes from the Long Branch bar, a longtime local institution; its original Edison bulbs were procured from the movie set of *A River Runs Through It*.

ABOVE: The homeowners chose to set the large industrial artwork, enamel laid down on aluminum by Timothy Tompkins, against the lichen-covered stone for a surprising juxtaposition. A cowhide lies under crossed beams and a glass light hand-crafted by a local artisan.

ABOVE: Polished aluminum chairs by Philippe Starck surround a table designed by the homeowner; the glass top rests on two concrete bases. The antique rug is from Santa Fe, while a dry sink found in Montana serves as a bar. An art piece made of strands of antique barbed wire collected from different regions of the country is echoed in the large lighting fixture made by Fire Mountain Forge.

FACING: The home's walls, pigmented plaster applied in two coats and then waxed, are inspired by French farmhouses and lend a warm glow. The kitchen features an English farmhouse sink, old wood pulleys found on the ranch, and a backsplash and breakfast bar wraparound made from parts of a rolled-out and flattened galvanized roof. The magnetized metal wall is the back of an old billboard—and still has the bullet holes to prove it.

FACING: Colonial American coverlets add color to the wall and bed and work well with the French fabrics. An old painted chest at the foot of the bed still bears the name of its original owners.

LEFT: The master suite opens onto a balcony, where the owner likes to play his electric keyboard. An artwork by Joe Amrhein, *The Screen Kiss*, is a nod to the couple's work.

BELOW: The husband/producer designed the bathroom with its free-standing tub, generously proportioned shower and dry-stacked, honed, tumbled slate. The sink is set in an antique top with steel legs. A skylight offers glimpses of passing clouds from the shower.

View of the bridge and "fire tower," which anchors the guest bed-rooms and houses the fire pole and staircase to the upper-level lookout. The stone masonry on the tower was a defining element that combined the varying scale, texture and color of Montana moss rock. Many of the feature stones (corners, window lintels) were selected by hand and viewed on-site before being installed.

Fresh Take on Traditional

Those who are drawn to the Mountain West today usually want a home that speaks to the great outdoors and references regional vernacular. But they also want clean lines, modern amenities and, most importantly, plenty of light. In short, they want a fresh take on traditional.

In response, accomplished architects combined with thoughtful clients are collaborating on homes throughout the region in a variety of expressions of the "new old." The most successful such homes are driven by clients who invest not only their passion but also their time in the project. Personal history plays an important role too. As the saying goes, the more you give, the more you get.

New York resident Kirk Davenport is a self-described frustrated architect. He studied architecture at Brown University, then considered attending Rhode Island School of Design for a graduate degree but went to law school instead. He had been involved with some renovations, but never a design-from-scratch project. When the time came to design a family home in Wyoming, then, he was more than a little involved.

As architect John Carney remembers it, "Kirk's wife said, 'I'm not sure you want to get this job. He's going to drive you crazy.' But we loved it. He gave us the opportunity to do a completely rustic house." Over the past twenty years, CLB Architects has designed everything from commercial and mixed-use projects to residences, including affordable housing. They recently completed the LEED-Platinum-rated Interpreter's Center at the Laurance S. Rockefeller Preserve. Their work for the most part has skewed modern, with a long-standing commitment to sustainability and a consistent emphasis on building site-sensitive structures in tune with the delicate ecosystem and natural beauty of the land.

The Davenports' property had natural beauty in spades. An elevated site situated up off the valley floor at the end of a road and backed by forest, it boasted sweeping views to the south toward the valley's famous Sleeping Indian mountain. Passionate backcountry skiers, the Davenports loved its proximity to Teton Pass as well as to the local saloon. "We have one foot in the wilderness and one foot in the little town of Wilson, and that seemed perfect to me," says Davenport.

With a shared vision for honest construction, sustained effort and the clients' unwavering commitment (manifested in weekly conference calls and the willingness to put work aside whenever a question came up), the project was completed in eighteen months. "I

was involved in every single decision," says Davenport. "I wanted the place to look like it had been here fifty years from the moment we moved in. We picked out all the timbers, all the stones, all the hardware. We never had any problem, any friction. And that includes all subs. We had a party in June for everyone who worked on the house. The guy who made the doors came all the way from Idaho with his family. Everyone was really proud of the job. People say construction is hard," he adds, "but for me, I was sad when it was done."

Ultimately the emotional investment paid off in a home that is as original as it is beautifully crafted. Unique features—a fire pole, a bridge to a tower housing the guest suite, a secret passageway accessed by a hidden door, and a ladder from the billiards room leading into the closet of the son's room above—add whimsy and fun. This balances the gravitas exuded by the house itself, which makes a significant architectural statement with its massive structural timbers, monumental stonework and visually arresting bridge. Lead architect Andy Ankeny, whose twin Jake Ankeny headed the team from Ankeny Construction Management, credits Davenport for pushing everyone involved to do his or her best work. "He was keen to challenge us in that way," Ankeny says. "He brought a level of fun to the project from the beginning."

On the opposite side of the Greater Yellowstone Ecosystem, an equally committed husband and wife were making their dream a reality with the help of Livingston-based Miller Architects and interior designer Laura Fedro. In this case, the Connecticut family was emotionally invested in the project due to their long history in the area.

Joe Roodell, project manager for Miller Architects, explains, "The wife's family had been Elkhorn Ranch guests since 1969. It had been their dream for the longest time to have their own place. Their children love the West; in fact, one son was living in Jackson, outfitting. Now the husband is retired, and they're moving to Montana as their primary residence."

The site is private, surrounded by forest. "What's great about this design is that it lends itself to that sense of discovery," says Roodell. "They're looking toward Ramshorn Peak and the Gallatin Range. In the distance is a meadow they've spent time in. In the living room they've set up a spotting scope to focus on the meadow for observing elk and other wildlife." The design process involved its own sense of discovery. Site visits to other Miller homes were key; they helped the architects get a feel for what the clients responded to volumetrically. By the end of the process they had decided on a three-bedroom house. A guest barn offers the opportunity for people to visit on their own without having to open up the main house.

Stylistically, their vision evolved throughout the process. Originally they had wanted a round-log home, but ultimately they chose a combination: hewn for the majority of interior and exterior walls, and round logs for rafters, trusses and posts. Using reclaimed materials from the area gave the home a sense of history. At the same time, the chosen materials would continue to weather gracefully through time.

Understandably, the couple didn't want the house to be too dark. They chose a lighter palette for the floors and trim, while Candace Tillotson-Miller designed a kitchen with open rafters and a dormer above to flood the space with light. Interior designer Laura Fedro says that with this group the design process was a pleasure. "The wife was involved in all the decisions. It was such a delight to talk with her about all the options available. Because of her love of the Elkhorn, she didn't want to re-create a turn-of-the-century cabin, but she wanted the comfort and familiarity of one. Specifically, she didn't want to live in a gigantic volume."

The house unfolds in a series of livable spaces with grand views. These begin at the front door. "The clients were clear that they wanted to be able to walk up to the main entry and see into the space that then looks out to the landscape," says Miller. "The effect it gives is one of transcending space."

The house features a generous but not over-scaled living room, dining area and kitchen; a serene master bedroom; a six-bed bunk room designed around a 1940s "Cowboy High Style" dresser; a cozy sitting room tucked behind the living room fireplace; and a killer mudroom with plenty of room for skis, snowshoes and fishing gear. Ample outdoor spaces include a screened porch with dining table and fireplace, and open porches and patios overlooking a pond and waterfall designed in collaboration with the husband. A passionate fly-fisherman, he wanted to have live water on the property; the pond then became a natural attractant for moose, elk and other fauna.

"The intention was for the house to be used and loved. It's a generational home. We chose good pieces, but nothing you can't put your feet on," says Fedro. "The wife is a voracious reader. She has two big swivel chairs facing a beautiful view to the south and east. It's important to have a workspace where you can collect things you need for your life. But she said all she needs is the big chair in front of the window."

A home designed by Miller Architects and built by On Site Management for a family with deep personal ties to the Big Sky area references dude ranch cabins and rustic living while being carefully integrated into a forested site that boasts dramatic mountain views

Uniquely Crafted

FACING: An east–facing porch has heavy timbers and exposed steel construction. Terraces were made from Montana limestone.

ABOVE: The house was situated between massive existing fir trees and uses a simple material palette to blend with the natural surroundings. The great room in the middle portion of the building has expansive windows fit within the timber construction to bridge the interior and exterior landscapes.

LEFT: The fireplace is the grounding element of the great room. Similar to the tower, individual pieces of Montana moss rock were hand-selected for their shape and texture for the hearth and mantel. The contractor sourced antique reclaimed firebrick to complete the timeless appearance.

FACING: The great room was conceived as a central gathering space that includes living room, dining room and kitchen. The room was designed to look like a renovated barn. Steel components and extended timber knee braces help balance the height and give the room a human scale.

FACING: The kitchen, with balcony above, has a flat ceiling with plaster finish to complement the wood throughout the rest of the space.

ABOVE: Interior designer Agnes Bourne, in collaboration with WRJ Designs, helped the clients bridge the divide between fresh and timeless through modern appliances, custom lighting, blackened steel, antique glass and retro-modern red-leather-topped stools.

RIGHT: A floating bridge links the staircase to the guest suite.

BELOW: Bedrooms were efficiently sized to accommodate the owners' large extended family. Daybeds were designed within window projections to increase the functional use and to bring more natural light into the rooms.

FACING: The main staircase near the entry lends a vertical scale to the space, and the upper windows serve as a lantern at night. The stairs are constructed from reclaimed fir timbers, with one serving as a bench. The lighting fixture was custom designed by the architect and interior designer Agnes Bourne.

FACING: The home office includes a door with antique glass and a desk built from a single walnut slab with a live edge.

ABOVE: The master bath has a Super White Quartzite vanity, Waterworks plumbing fixtures and reclaimed wood millwork.

Sense of Discovery

ABOVE LEFT: Square logs suggest timelessness, while extensive use of local stone grounds the building to its site.

ABOVE RIGHT: A screened porch makes the most of indoor–outdoor living in the best rustic tradition.

ABOVE: The lower media room provides a quiet getaway to watch a film or play billiards.

FACING: The great room is a central gathering space for the family, with upholstered seating, a live-edge table by Brandner Design and a custom wool carpet by Tai Ping. Views of Ramshorn Peak dominate the graciously scaled paned windows.

A Corbin Bronze chandelier centers the dining area, while a Ted Waddell painting hangs on the hand-finished plaster wall.

FACING: The light-filled mudroom with its oversized upholstered ottoman offers ample storage for summer and winter sports gear.

ABOVE: A bunkroom takes its design cues from an antique "cowboy high-style" chest of drawers, a gift from the wife's parents.

ABOVE: Laura Fedro Interiors specified the Victoria and Albert tub for its depth and dual ends. It's the perfect place to soak after a day on the slopes. Custom cabinets built by Crown Creations and a warm, rich mohair runner finish the space.

FACING: Layers of textures create a comfortable bedroom retreat.

Authentic Rustic

The house is dwarfed by its forest surroundings and anchored to its site on the edge of a pond by massive stone chimneys and the timeless solidity of heavy timbers. It is designed to blend in and to speak to its surroundings—certainly an appropriate response to the outsized grandeur of its setting near the Snake River in Jackson Hole. Its interiors, though, vie with the Tetons for their ability to stop motion. An expression of the long-standing vision of two collectors, here a unique cache of one-of-a-kind treasures is displayed in a home whose honesty in construction is equaled by the authenticity of its artworks.

The homeowners, according to Los Angeles–based interior designer Elizabeth Dinkel, are both passionate collectors. An entertainment lawyer married to an actress, the couple had lived in another home in Wyoming and already owned a trove of museum-quality Native American artifacts—including vessels, beadwork, clothing, good luck charms, blankets and instruments—before beginning the design of this house. Their interests spanned worlds. The actress, for instance, was a connoisseur of majolica, while the husband was drawn to prehistoric pottery. He, a fisherman, collected antique creels, while she, with her interest in design and color, collected textiles. Together they were drawn to truly special finds, such as a Joseph Heinrich Arts & Crafts–era presentation silver punch bowl with bronze Indian heads; an antique railroad model; and Tiffany stained-glass windows. In their new home, a perfectly preserved 1930s Old Town canoe hangs from the ceiling in an upstairs gallery.

Without a doubt, the heart of the home is its barrel-vaulted great room and, anchoring it, a massive totem pole that speaks of another world. The 26-foot-tall hand-carved artwork, circa 1880, of the Haida tribe is just one of many museum-quality pieces on display. Terry Winchell, owner of Fighting Bear Antiques in Jackson Hole, was involved with the project from its inception and had advised the homeowners prior to that. Winchell and Dinkel both describe a process in which the home was designed to accommodate the owners' collection. The totem pole, given its height, weight and consequent engineering issues, constituted the most significant challenge. It was worth every effort, asserts Winchell, for its impact is immeasurable. "That totem pole has had another life," he says. "It lay in the basement of a museum in Boston for 90 years with water dripping on it. It's the real thing, and it sets the tone when you walk in. Very few early totems have survived. It defines a collection when someone has a focal point like that."

Stephen Tobler, a Portland, Oregon, architect previously based in Jackson Hole, designed the home that would showcase these spectacular artifacts. He was able to balance the vision of the clients and the complexities of their art collection with the unique demands of the area, such as topography, wildlife and winter snow loads. "Originally, the owners were envisioning a more modernist twist on a ranch-influenced structure," Tobler recalls, "for instance, large panes of glass with no mullions, to open up the view. Their reaction was to try to get more exterior exposure into the house, but sometimes the quality of space in these cozy cabins with a womb-like atmosphere becomes desirable. Initially they wanted clean, modern lines, but they also they wanted it to be of the West." Thus, over multiple design iterations the house evolved into a more ranch-influenced design with a vintage feel.

Traditional rustic architecture carries with it its own set of constraints, such as smaller apertures, which result in less natural light. The question for the architect became how to maintain the quality of the space while maximizing light, and how to accommodate the needs of the clients while mitigating the volume of a larger home. The house was constructed using post-and-beam construction and boasts unusual double-height vaulted-ceiling rooms built using ship-construction techniques. The steel strapping is both functional and traditional; it has a long history, dating back to Amish barns and shipbuilding. Visually, it speaks to authenticity. Says Tobler, "There was rigor on our part for finding historic precedent, but rather than just copy we would say, where would we go with this as a next step? Historically, glass was scarce, and apertures were small for both structural and practical reasons. But jump 100 years and people want modern kitchens and beautiful views. There are things we have to do, such as add steel, to make it all work. Yet we still have the romantic view of a little western cabin."

Fortuitously, the result is not only site-appropriate and very functional but also extremely conducive to displaying the owners' art. The home has the feel of a traditional log house. Wood walls create a dignified backdrop for the Native American pieces, while the bright colors of the beadwork stand out against the more somber tones of the house. In some key wall spaces, such as the kitchen, the owners selected rich colors to create vibrancy and to offset the preponderance of wood.

Dinkel says the ultimate result was the product of close collaboration between the clients, Tobler and herself. The building team at Ankeny Construction Management was invaluable, as was expertise lent by the mechanical engineers, the property's caretaker and rustic antiques expert Winchell. "The home is in the woods, tucked away and built on a pond, where it blends into the natural environment. The clients wanted a backdrop to showcase their collections, they wanted to feature the natural environment and they wanted something apropos to where they live in Wyoming," Dinkel explains. "The architecture speaks to local traditions without having all the expected elements."

Tobler says his task was to create an appropriate showcase for the art while creating some consistency of detailing so the design would hold up over time. In this respect, as in so many others, the home is an unqualified success. But form and function have to work together, and for Winchell, a home is only as good as its components. To him, the monumental totem pole—anchoring the house, as the Grand Teton anchors the nearby mountain range—makes the grandest statement where it stands, at the heart of the home and as a testament to its authenticity.

A traditional post-and-beam home near the Snake River and Teton Mountains marries form and function as a repository for an extraordinary collection of western art and antiques and Native American artifacts.

ABOVE: European antler mounts, red fabric on original Thomas Molesworth furniture and a vintage lamp create a camp-like feel.

FACING: French wrought-iron sconces cast a warm glow over an 1880s French fruitwood cabinet. The homeowners collected the vintage Native American baskets and textiles over a long period.

FACING: The great room, with its prominent structural timbers and functional iron strapping, is a showcase of museum-quality furniture, art, saddles, pottery, textiles and Native American artifacts.

ABOVE: In the breakfast nook, the owner's collection of majolica stands out against a deep green wall. A red leather banquette and custom hand-glazed Ann Sacks tiles around the fireplace create a cozy feel.

LEFT: The kitchen, with glass cabinets from Christopher Peacock, variegated green tile backsplash and playful elk "mount," was built to accommodate a crowd.

RIGHT: A museum-quality model train and black-and-white Edward S. Curtis photographs occupy pride of place at the stairwell.

BELOW: Vintage chaps in rustic frames hang above the bed, which is simply covered with an old Pendleton blanket. The flower-motif rug of hair-on cowhide is from The Rug Company in London.

FACING: The upstairs gallery, with its Arts & Crafts lighting and bronze sculpture, displays a perfectly pre-served 1930s Old Town canoe.

FACING: The double-height master bedroom utilized shipbuilding tech-niques in the construction of the ceiling. The green wall creates a foundation for the vibrant colors found in Native American artifacts.

ABOVE: Subdued hues, wood floors and ceilings and a Waterworks copper-clad slipper tub create a timeless refuge.

The Little Lost Cabin, situated in a broad expanse on a conservation parcel in northern Idaho, sits at the base of a small rise. It overlooks Summit Creek, providing a top-water view upstream toward the southeast, with the Lemhi Range beyond.

Sustainable Rustic

Sustainability may be a convenient buzzword, but it's really just another phrase for treading lightly on the land. And when every built structure quite literally leaves a footprint, treading lightly becomes a choice, whether conscious or not.

In two extraordinary cabins, thoughtful building is taken to its logical end point: site appropriateness, modest scaling, ultra efficiency. There is no better way to appreciate the great outdoors, it seems, than by inhabiting a conscientiously conceived indoors.

Architect Clark Stevens of New West Land Company was tasked with designing a three-season dwelling on 3,000 barely accessible and mostly untreed—but wildly beautiful—acres in Idaho. The land, purchased by a conservation developer then immediately protected by easement, had end-of-road appeal, live water, prime fly-fishing and spectacular 360-degree views of the Lemhi and Lost River mountain ranges.

The Michigan- and Harvard-trained architect originally came west to pursue his passion—"large landscapes, small dwellings"—and this assignment certainly lived up to his expectations. Stevens based his design on an old calving shed with an offset granary on the Gallatin River that he used to pass on his way to go fishing. "I love that building composition," he says, "but what's wrong with vernacular architecture intended for animal or grain storage is there's no natural light and no views. But to simply punch windows in walls for that purpose detracts from the essential solidity of these structures. Instead, what we try to do is leave voids between otherwise continuous forms, respecting the integrity of the walls and rooflines—kind of a vernacular modernism."

Critical to this approach is precise placement of the building to optimize the experience of the place and the function of the living environment. The house was built off the grid, so energy use needed to be minimalized. The architect sited the cabin to get as much winter sun as possible while minimizing exposure to the summer sun. The porch was carefully oriented to get the most sun during the low winter light.

Although the structure seems exposed, its placement was carefully considered. The cabin is backed by a knoll, which provides some protection from the wind while keeping the cabin open to the light. Says Stevens, "It's subtle but it helps anchor the dwelling to the site."

At 700 square feet, the open-plan interior features exposed beams, large window walls, designated spaces for cooking, eating and relaxing, a master bedroom, a sleeping loft accessible by ladder and, in a moment of grace, a stand-alone bathtub with a glorious view. In pursuit of efficiency and economy, the cabin is furnished with inexpensive lighting fixtures, a simple, logo-free two-burner gas stove, and on-demand hot water. But its most responsible feature is invisible. The cabin is "the oldest kind of pre-fab," says Stevens. The logs were cut and stacked off-site then unstacked, moved and reassembled on-site. Interestingly, it's also mobile. A special steel frame enables the whole thing to be picked up and dragged, skidded or put on a flatbed and moved, should someone change his or her mind down the road.

Many owners do, in fact, modify their ideas substantially once they've had a chance to get to know their land. When Todd Thomson first conceived his family's Montana retreat, the idea was to build a cabin that would ultimately become the guesthouse to a generously scaled main house. After several seasons with his full family in residence, though, the place had worked its magic; for the time being at least, their compact home suits all their needs.

The Thomson's 1,800-square-foot cabin was designed and supervised during construction by Daniel Turvey of Dan Joseph Architects and built and managed by Todd Thesing and Rob McRae of Highline Partners, each one in constant and close collaboration with Thomson. "We worked very hard to create something small, unique and intimate, with a family feeling," Thomson says. There is no wasted space and the home is extremely efficient. The small scale was a moderate challenge compared to Thompson's loftier goal of building a LEED Platinum–certified home. If they succeeded, it would be the first of its kind in southwest Montana, and one of the only such structures in the entire state. This was important to Thompson, a lifelong outdoorsman and avid conservationist.

Although building a cabin with such a dramatically small footprint was a new process for many of the people involved, they immediately set about educating themselves as to the seven measures of home performance defined by the LEED process: location and linkages; sustainable sites; water efficiency; indoor environmental quality; energy and atmosphere; homeowner awareness; and innovation and design. There are as many as 100 variables to be considered and monitored in pursuit of certification; the team's response was to sign up for educational seminars, read up and dig in. "We were on board 150 percent," recalls contractor Thesing.

The overall master plan would incorporate water features designed and located by the architect. Thomson's iconic childhood memory was spending summers fishing on his grandfather's homestead on the banks of the McKenzie River in Oregon. His 22-acre Montana parcel had two streams, the starting point for a network of waterways that would ultimately consist of four ponds connected by streams and waterfalls. In addition to the ponds' visual and auditory aesthetics, their use as habitat for fish, attraction to wildlife, and potential for swimming, they had a higher goal: providing enough geothermal mass to heat the cabin and, possibly, a large home during the winter, and cool each during the summer. They dug the main pond to a depth of 25 feet, where the temperature is constant at 55 degrees, and installed geothermal heat-exchange plates.

From the magnificent to the mundane, every detail was considered, resulting in an array of solar panels (which generate 20% of the home's energy needs) fixed to the horse barn's corrugated tin roof (reclaimed, of course). A gray-water reclamation system captures household water and reuses it for toilets and drip irrigation; other energy-reducing technologies include dual-flush toilets, compact fluorescent light bulbs, Energy Star appliances, and, in the barn, a composting toilet. Reclaimed and local materials were used throughout the project, while extreme recycling and minimization of construction waste were prioritized.

The structure, though constructed using today's modern means and methods, takes its outward visual inspiration from classic Parkitecture, exhibiting timeless appeal through use of dove-tailed timbers, dry-stacked stone, standing dead log beams and columns, and reclaimed wood flooring, rafters and beams. Hand-crafted interiors convey warmth and celebrate local craftsmanship, particularly in the loft stairway with antler balustrade, a major focal point in the home. Generously scaled windows (triple-paned for energy efficiency) open onto views of Pioneer Mountain and beyond.

There are some particular keys to making a smaller home successful. "It must understand its place in the environment," explains architect Turvey. "How does it address the water? The trees? The views?

"It's like a three-legged stool. First, there needs to be an expression of structure; people enjoy the sight of beams, columns and connections. Second, a sense of transparency: you need to see in and around and through, while still protecting inhabitants from the elements. And lastly, great architecture must be site-specific; it is essential that the built response feel as though it truly belongs, that it is uniquely and organically rooted in its place. Architecture and site must have a meaningful dialog with one another, to speak back and forth 'til each is inseparable from the whole."

The home is successful in every sense, even winning *Mountain Living*'s "Most Responsible Residence" award. And despite the special challenges of designing at 8,000 feet for heavy snow load in an active seismic zone, it did earn LEED-platinum certification. The cabin's cozy warmth and intimacy, its relationship to the pond and landscape, and its handmade character all combine to create a family home whose very restrained size is one of its most compelling features.

"For me it's a more modest way of treading on the environment. I don't want to say it's for everyone," says Thomson, "but for a lot of people, if they had time to focus on it, they'd do something along the lines of what we've done here. There's a sense of calm when something sits so well in the environment and is so comfortable. In the eastern world they would call it feng shui."

Clark Stevens, designer of Idaho's Little Lost Cabin, agrees with that philosophy. "If you build what belongs there, it happens more easily than if you don't."

The seeming simplicity of a traditional square-log cabin of weathered materials belies its technological forwardness. A large pond, dug to a depth of 25 feet for consistent temperatures, houses geothermal heat-exchange plates.

Little Lost Cabin

ABOVE: A ring of peaks surrounds the cabin, seen here from the north, where entry is sheltered by a small porch at the glazed dogtrot between the low-slung shed form and the tower-like granary. Openings are limited on this side to the framing of key views while sheltering the cabin's interior from northern exposures.

FACING: Small cabin, big view: porch seating faces east and south, toward warm sun and rising trout.

FACING: The diagonal arrangement of the porch with the main interior space blurs the boundary between inside and out. The porch adds depth to the living space and shades the primary vistas without adding too much to the structure's overall square footage.

RIGHT: A heavy timber-framed mezzanine provides a secondary sleeping space while lending an intimate scale to the dining and cooking areas.

FACING: The freestanding tub was given a prime location in the loft–like open plan of the cabin to offer sunrise and sunset views. The soundproof wall behind the tub uses plywood bands and Homasote sound board to continue the horizontal stacking of the structural logs.

ABOVE: The bed is positioned for nighttime viewing of the constellations yet is set in a niche (created by the tub and water closet enclosure) that creates a sleep–friendly scale of enclosure.

Headwaters Camp

ABOVE LEFT: Headwaters Camp, a haven for wildlife located on the edge of the Greater Yellowstone Ecosystem, was the first LEED Platinum–certified home in southwestern Montana.

ABOVE RIGHT: A modestly scaled main house situated amidst a series of interconnected ponds, streams, and waterfalls is augmented by a working barn.

LEFT: Large timbers, stacked stone and traditional western furnishings combine ruggedness with comfort for a sense of refuge.

FACING: Interior Designer Erika Jennings of Sisson Designs incorporated recycled items whenever possible. The green kitchen cabinets are actually two halves of a turn-of-the-century step-back piece found in Bozeman.

FACING: Built-ins create extra space in modestly scaled homes, while unadorned windows enhance the indoor-outdoor experience.

RIGHT: A wooden trough sink and corrugated metal sliding door creates a rustic retreat. The sink is an Indonesian dough bowl that once held slippers.

From its elevation at 8,000 feet, the Colorado
home of painter William Matthews looks to the
south toward Pike's Peak. Glimpsed through
the French doors of the kitchen, a white-tailed
deer stands next to a large bronze urn Matthews
brought back from a trip to southern India.

Artistic License

f a home is a reflection of those who dwell in it, an artist's home is a dramatic expression of his influences, experiences, and passions. This is particularly true of acclaimed watercolor painter William Matthews, whose Colorado home, studio and office serve as galleries—not for his own work, but for his extensive and ever-evolving collections.

Although Matthews admits he's close to stepping over the line of being overwhelmed by belongings, he cannot stop collecting. "The reality is, as an artist and somebody who has a fairly refined aesthetic sense, I'm often drawn to really beautiful things," he explains. He is drawn to paintings and drawings, especially by watercolorists who have inspired him. He's drawn to objects such as furniture and instruments, some of which hang on walls, some of which are kept out and played. He collects Navajo textiles voraciously, as well as porcelain signage from the '20s and '30s. Also catching his discerning eye are calligraphy and Chinese scholars' materials, like brush pots made of exotic woods; optical equipment, old cameras and viewing devices like stereoscopic recorders; medical equipment; fossils; and thousands of books. "I have more than 100 hats," says Matthews, "many of which have been given to me. I consider them incredibly valuable and important."

For this artist-collector, whose passions range from vintage antler furniture to esoteric musical instruments, the hard part is figuring out how to live with all those things. While it helps that he has a 10,000-square-foot warehouse in Denver, which serves as office, gallery, display space, frame shop and storage unit, he still has a need to be surrounded by items that inform and inspire his art.

"When I'm displaying things," he says, "I don't have the luxury of going highly minimal: for instance, one wall with one painting, or a table with three small pieces. Our house is fairly cluttered. We might have a concertina mixed with Japanese woodblocks also mixed with ceramics. My wife and I have some rooms we try not to allow to get too cluttered, but we still have piles of books because we're usually both reading twelve different things at once."

In most homes the result would be disarray, but Matthews' artistic eye and meticulous attention to detail translates to refined, richly layered interiors. In the living room alone, there are George Carlson bronzes, kachinas, pots and baskets and old mahogany boxes and English watercolor sets. Antiques include an 1830s William IV architect's desk, a Windsor chair, and leather furniture. There's a Kiowa cradleboard, a Thomas Jefferson bust, a Shaker bucket, a Scandinavian spinning wheel, an Irish potato spade, a Japanese carved eagle and eaglet, a red deer antler rack, a diaphonic accordion, and a pair of lights made out of call horns from a fire brigade. Artwork includes a Fritz Scholder acrylic, a Frank Schoonover bucking horse gouache, a 15th-century German Renaissance painting and a Frederick Waugh oil painting that belonged to his grandfather.

Each room in Matthews' house is a repository for a variety of art and artifacts. For the artist, these individual items serve as catalysts for his own work. "Some of these links can be inspirational in ways you don't expect," he says.

Matthews has had a colorful life: the son of educated, artistic parents, he dropped out of high school to pursue careers in music and art, briefly attended art school, took a trip to Europe and ended up staying five years. "Through all that early part of my life," Matthews recalls, "it really was about collecting material and interest, and getting an idea of what's out there to come back to the West with a broad view." And although Matthews continues to travel, and collect, he also finds all the inspiration he needs right at home.

An art collector's home is also an expression of influences and a source of inspiration—though in this case for living, rather than for creating art. A thoughtfully curated collection of works speaks volumes of the person who created it. For one New York resident who has lived and traveled all over the world, his Montana ranch constitutes the ideal setting to explore place-based art. For this collector, it offers an opportunity to indulge his passion for fine art and antiques, particularly sculpture and photography, in a setting that is simultaneously rustic and refined.

An international businessman who buys art for various homes, his goal is to curate collections that are deeply meaningful yet site-appropriate. He discovered his Montana escape, a small working ranch with existing buildings, in 1992. A series of projects undertaken by JFL & Associates saw renovation of a lodge building and reconstruction and realignment of other buildings, including a barn and garage.

The ranch lies in a small valley near Paradise Valley, just north of Yellowstone National Park. It is bisected by a stream and smothered by mountains and forest. The collector had spent a few days in a helicopter searching before finding the right property, a compound of western buildings. The original lodge building, circa 1949, was in bad shape. He had it dismantled, reconfigured and put back together. All the buildings were redone, reinforced with steel and clad with timber to keep the feeling of the original structures.

A lifelong art enthusiast, he likes having works that speak to the presence of their environment. "My art collection in New York is very contemporary," he says. "I don't have a single piece of western art in New York, so when I go to Montana I really appreciate it."

The art, some of which was commissioned, is a vibrant mixture of black-and-white photography, both old (Edward S. Curtis prints of Native Americans) and contemporary; paintings in various media; framed vintage posters; both indoor and outdoor sculpture; and whimsical pieces such as small Black Forest-type antler mounts, contemporary painted totem poles, and white ceramic molds of hands, made for a glove factory, that he found antiquing. The homeowner, who enjoys interior design as a hobby, selected all the furnishings as well: a mixture of vintage Arts & Crafts furniture and lamps, wildlife mounts, antiquarian books, traditional leather-covered sofas, and antique European and Middle Eastern textiles. He has been collecting for half a century and has an unerring eye. "Usually when something goes up," he says, "it never comes down."

Both collectors have traveled the world over and lived abroad, one working in the business world while collecting, one painting while collecting. For Matthews, his artistic exploration of the rural West, sustained over a period of decades, has resulted in international acclaim and major exhibitions. For the collector, his art defines the refuges that help sustain his work and inform his inner life.

For both artist and collector, one's home—and its relationship to the exterior (the surrounding landscape), the interior (its art and furnishings) and its occupant—is a living display that speaks to the soul.

Fiberglass and resin Cowboys & Indians sculptures by Tel Aviv–born artist Yoram Wolberger stand guard over the entrance to a Paradise Valley ranch in Montana.

A Broad View

ABOVE LEFT: The painter, influenced by growing up amidst Bay Area Arts & Crafts and Bernard Maybeck architecture, chose to construct Shingle style; its aesthetic works well in the Colorado mountains, and it ages beautifully. Matthews designed and built the 11-foot-long teak dining table to accommodate large gatherings by the outdoor fireplace.

ABOVE RIGHT: In the summer, when the fireplace is inactive, Matthews leans some of his collectible instruments—including a 1903 Fairbanks Whyte Laydie banjo and an electric bouzouki he made himself from an old Danelectro 12-string—against the screen. "I like having things around," he says. A small George Carlson sculpture, a California Indian gambling tray, a Wendy Artin watercolor, African arm masks and a sign from a Japanese paint shop complete the vignette.

Both fireplace and ceiling of Matthews' living room reveal an Arts & Crafts influence. Books, textiles and comfortable leather furniture—including a giant ottoman purchased from a Ralph Lauren storage warehouse—invite relaxation and conviviality. Unique pieces, such as a heavily burled console table crafted by the late Mike Patrick of New West Furniture, pewter lamps made from turn–of–the–century firemen's call horns, and a French–Canadian canoe purchased at a French flea market, add interest and individuality.

RIGHT: Beaded moccasins, a 7-string banjo and Native American textiles stacked in an antique rice basket purchased from a rice shop in a small village in China are displayed in the front hall. William Matthews has painted the Gamble Ranch granary almost a hundred times.

FACING: A pine desk with old tools, an eighteenth-century Pennsylvanian Windsor chair, Northeast Woodlands Indian paddles and a watercolor by American painter John McCoy furnish a quiet, well-lit nook on a landing.

FACING: A vintage German antler table and a work by Irish landscape painter Paul Henry comprise a bedroom tableau.

ABOVE: Pages in the guest book are signed by fellow artists Buckeye Blake and Teal Blake and by the artist's son.

LEFT: A display of drawings includes works by Maynard Dixon, E. Irving Couse and the original artwork for the frontispiece of Edgar Payne's classic book *The Composition of Outdoor Painting.*

Vibrant Mixture

FACING: A stone water feature with meandering trough echoes the natural waterways found in the nearby wilderness and speaks to the ruggedness of the home's stone walls and mountain setting.

LEFT: Folk art references mix freely with more modern pieces in this collector's home.

ABOVE: Elemental materials and a modestly scaled door belie the grandeur of the setting and the home's extensive trove of art. The owner has been collecting for almost fifty years.

LEFT: The collector chose not just the art but the furnishings, opting for a warm, comfortable and somewhat eclectic interior.

FACING: Modernist totem poles and black-and-white photographs furnish a hallway of stone, glass and beams. The homeowner collects antique rugs from the Mideast and Europe, vintage posters and antiquarian books, as well as photography by Edward S. Curtis and Mexican artist Wouter Deruytter.

FACING: Brown–stained wainscoting, Arts & Crafts furniture, vintage suit–cases and a collection of athletic team and group photographs from the 1920s and '30s lend the bedroom a retro feel.

ABOVE: A classic white tub and wainscoting create fresh appeal in a bath–room. The life–sized hands are rubber glove molds the owner found in an antique store.

Eastern white cedar and hemlock were left unfinished after careful consideration of how they would weather and oxidize. Doors to the living area open wide to create an indoor–outdoor room yet can close up tight in a storm.

Lakeside Rustic

The classic rustic vernacular expressed in nineteenth-century Adirondack Great Camps speaks to the American psyche. Their lake's-edge siting; use of indigenous logs, shingle and stone; their evolution and expansion over time; and their wilderness settings created a sense of timelessness. They offered a serenity sorely needed as a respite from the clamor of the city.

When the Montana-based Pearson Design Group was approached to conceive a Great Camp-inspired project on a private lake in upstate New York, they were transfixed by the notion of adapting their hallmark western regional style to an eastern setting. They were also intrigued by the intellectual puzzle of building a timeless camp that appeared to evolve over decades while still meeting modern demands. Scale and appropriateness to landscape and region were the dual lenses through which every detail was considered.

The property was a thousand-acre dairy farmstead whose centerpiece is a spring-fed lake that ultimately feeds into the Hudson River. Of several existing structures, it was the smallest—not much more than a decrepit shack—that became the designers' reference point for appropriate scale.

The clients, a film director, a writer, and their three children, led with their creativity, knowledge and a passion for rustic places, antiques and camps. They had a strong vision and a desire for authenticity. Architect Larry Pearson says the team's goal was to reference the Great Camps without attempting to build in the Adirondack style. "We focused on what could have been built in a place like this, what might have been constructed by a family in an era when access was by train or horse. We took our clues from the vernacular style of the region. We wanted it to be original yet traditional."

Central to the plan and adhering to regional precedent was the concept of multiple dwellings serving distinct purposes. The stone and timber main house is situated on a knoll, with a view over the lake to the surrounding densely wooded hills. Its reclaimed timber and two-foot-thick walls ground it to the land and region. Below it, integrated into the lake's edge, is the boathouse, open to the water in the Adirondack tradition for boat storage. The cabin-like structure includes a bedroom inspired by old-time sleeping porches and features clever innovations for indoor-outdoor living. Integrated stonework along and underneath the lake ground the building and provide ledges for swimming and diving, while a dock offers ample space for sunbathing, loading a boat for an outing or contemplating the hush at twilight. The third building, a pool house/cabana with

covered patio, is a streamlined structure of reclaimed wood and stone, with simple, light interiors and a central sliding barn door.

The project was designed by Larry Pearson and Pearson Design Group Principal Justin Tollefson, who was architect and coordinator of the project over a five-year period. Stonework that anchors the compound was created by master masons Thomas Schiel and Christopher Gregory, in collaboration with landscape architect Judy Murphy of Old Farm Nursery in Lakeville, Connecticut. Kristen Panitch, of Kristen Panitch Interiors in Los Angeles, helped oversee the project throughout the process, from its inception through programming to finished spaces. Balsamo Interior Design and Cayle Design in New York were involved in selecting many of the unique finishes, with resident property managers Ruel and Aileen Jusi supervising implementation.

The architects went to extraordinary lengths to stay within the realm of appropriateness. More than half the volume of the main house, or Lake Cabin, is built into the hillside and hidden from view. The architects designed the structures so they'd appear to be uninsulated; their thin roofs, visible wall cavities, single glazed windows and exposed rafters assured that at first glance the buildings would not look contemporary. In this way the designers achieved spectacularly the goal of timelessness. The idea, explains Pearson, was that the compound "should have a sense of being built over time rather than having been executed in one vision. It should have a rich palette, with overlapping sensibilities. In the Great Camps, you had a sixty- or eighty-year time line." Thus, he explains, "the stonework, the siding, the rafters—they all shift as you move from building to building."

Tollefson refers to this understated approach as "architecture with a lower-case 'a,' architecture without ego. The effect is that it looks 150 years old and took a generation to build."

The boathouse, in particular, was an exercise in restraint and is a model for indoor-outdoor living. The little bedroom at the end "juts over the water and has glass walls," says Pearson. "The windows open up so that you hear the water lapping against the footings. The effect is like being in your own boat in the lake. To access that bedroom, you walk through the covered dock, which obviously has water in it.

The hallway *is* the water, and it forces you to move through the land-scape. There's intimacy in both scale and connection to nature. It's not meant to be separated from the environment."

Of course, the main prerogative of a design with multiple dwellings is that it forces residents outdoors into nature in all its glory, in all weather and in all seasons. And no matter how beautiful or how comfortable the accommodations, that is exactly the point.

A compound of new structures inspired by traditional Adirondack camps was designed by Pearson Design Group to speak to a hilly lakeside site. In keeping with regional precedence, the architects worked hard to incorporate local materials and minimize massing. The main home's bedrooms hide beneath a living roof, while locally quarried granite helps tie the structures to the land and create a cohesive whole. A porch with removable windows and a fanciful antique stove overlooks the lake view.

Granite edges the meandering curve
of the shoreline, linking the fire pit
area to the open boathouse.

FACING: The windows of the boathouse kitchen and serving bar operate on a cleverly designed rope and pulley system.

ABOVE: A dock that extends over the surface of the lake literally spans the divide between land and water. Canoes, a rowboat and wooden paddle board at the ready make the most of the lakeside setting and encourage spontaneous adventures.

LEFT: Working gas lamps help create a romantic setting for meals at the long harvest table.

True timber trusses and purloins and 20-inch-thick stone walls attest to the structural authenticity of the Lake Cabin. Montana blacksmith Bill Moore made the windows over-looking the porch. Master masons Thomas Schiel and Christopher Gregory created the extraordinary stonework in the buildings and at the water's edge, and the stone stairways and bridges that serve as connective elements throughout the compound.

FACING: Antique lighting fixtures, open shelving, hinged windows with chain stays and ceiling planks distressed with plaster lend character to the kitchen.

ABOVE: Traditionally built cabinetry is finished with steel nails; the built-in table is vintage.

LEFT: Antique transom windows allow light into an interior bath-room. The sink, fixtures, lights, mirrors, tiles and glass with steel wire set into the door are all antique.

FACING: A cozy bedroom with leaded windows has curtained bunk beds, a granite window ledge, a cork floor, and gin mats covering the ceiling. Strap hinges and other forged hardware were made by blacksmith Mark Emig, with additional hardware by Historic Housefitters.

FACING: A sleeping porch on one end of the boathouse is simply fur-nished and surrounded by water.

LEFT: In the master bedroom, tucked under a living roof and overlooking the pond, stone details carry through from outside.

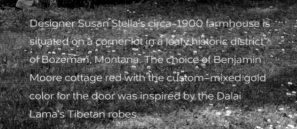

Designer Susan Stella's circa-1900 farmhouse is situated on a corner lot in a leafy historic district of Bozeman, Montana. The choice of Benjamin Moore cottage red with the custom-mixed gold color for the door was inspired by the Dalai Lama's Tibetan robes.

Dual Expressions

Susan M. Stella is a stylist, a fine art photographer, an interior designer, and an inveterate traveler. Trained in painting and printmaking, she brings her eye for color, balance, proportion and textural contrasts to projects ranging from retail spaces to private dwellings in Montana, California and beyond. In two very different homes—one small, one large; one an adobe casita, one a vintage farmhouse—discovered at different stages in her life, she marries her own history and aesthetic to that of each house and its locale. In each case, the result is a thoughtfully curated sequence of spaces, each of which exudes serenity.

"I look at a space like an installation," Stella explains. "It's about color, shapes, light and dark. It's like a three-dimensional painting."

The Montana house, a home for Stella, her dogs and her daughter during her daughter's middle school years, was a straightforward move. The circa-1900 farmhouse, located in a designated historic district of a vibrant college town, had good bones and plenty of room.

The house had been lightly modernized. On the first floor, instead of small, dark Victorian-era rooms it had a large, open, airy room filled with light. Stella's first moves were to redo the kitchen and install tall double-hung windows. Happily, when she went to update the floors, she pulled up the existing tiles and uncovered beautiful old fir floors. She replaced vinyl doors with the original wood doors, which she found stored in the basement, as well as the old hardware. The house had been painted in an array of intense colors that lacked the tonal quality to work together aesthetically. Stella painted most of the interior in Benjamin Moore White Dove, then chose a dark green trim inspired by the Shaker palette. Shaker minimalism, in fact, inspired much of the redesign and lends a serenity and elegance throughout.

The white walls with green trim create a unifying background. In the kitchen, the cabinets were also painted Shaker green. The fir wainscoting was finished in oil, as were the wood floors in the rest of the house, to allow them to age to a deep orange tone. Stella chose orange Marmoleum flooring in the kitchen in keeping with the palette of the rest of the home's warm-toned fir floors.

Clearly, color has the potential to make the biggest impact in the refurbishing of an historic home. "Changing the interior and exterior colors and restoring elements to their original design made a huge difference in the house," says the designer. For the exterior, she referenced the traditional farmhouse with a rich red color contrasted with a high-gloss black oil enamel trim. The effect is sharp, clean and contemporary, yet is still true to the historic nature of the home and its neighborhood.

Stella had fun with furnishings, mixing items she already owned with new-found treasures. An oversized teak dining table, previously anchoring her storefront loft in Venice, California, fit perfectly into the open ground floor living space of the Bozeman house, complemented by an antique New Mexican turquoise hutch she had bought years before. She shopped for furnishings in local antiques stores in Montana, and purchased modern pieces like the Noguchi lamps and coffee table, a Saarinen womb chair, and side tables from Stephanie Sandson's design gallery, Shack Up.

Stella is not afraid to mix periods and regions, to great effect. "Mixing periods was a fun integration of traditional turn-of-the-century farmhouse vernacular with contemporary design. I started playing around with adding modern pieces. The house was open and airy and took well to mixing different periods. In bringing the modern into the traditional and working with the architecture of the region, I was also trying to accent history. Rumor has it that the house was once a boarding house. There were funny patches on the floor, which made it all the more interesting."

As life in Montana settled into a rhythm, Stella found herself increasingly drawn to New Mexico. She had always dreamed of having a place there, a getaway where she could be creative. She eventually found the perfect opportunity in a small adobe in Tesuque, a time-stands-still village outside Santa Fe. "It was a great little house," she said. "I was instantly intrigued by it. It was hand-built by the family that was living down the dirt road. There was an organic quality to it that really appealed to my love of buildings made of earthy materials."

The house was in need of new stucco, a new roof and a reworking of the interior space and details. Inside she built a kitchen counter/table made of adobe bricks topped with a five-inch-thick ponderosa pine top. She replaced the doors and the door frames and bull-nosed the frames. She plastered, pulled out wall heaters and created niches in their place. The thick adobe walls around the windows had thinly tiled windowsills; she ripped those out and installed three-inch-thick Ponderosa pine sills to match the window lintels that were original to the house. A fiberglass built-in shower unit was replaced with traditional Talavera Mexican tiles. The kitchen and living area, where there is a beautiful kiva fireplace, was in the same open, albeit small, space. To utilize the volume of the open room, she designed and built an adobe *banco*, a bench built into the wall that wraps around the corner of the room. This traditional New Mexican design allows a small space to be used more efficiently.

Ultimately her daughter went off to school and Stella moved to New Mexico full time. "It was a huge downsizing process," she recalls. "The challenge was where to put everything, how to use the space and how to get a feeling of some openness. I came to the conclusion that it's really good to have built-ins. In working with small spaces you have to be very careful. I've taken three trips to Morocco and love the architecture; it's of the earth and is a strong influence. Their architecture incorporates built-in seating as part of the traditional design."

The result, she says, is a New Mexican aesthetic with a North African feeling. "In North Africa they generally work with organic materials," she explains. "I tried to stay with organic in this house. I used wrought iron rather than steel. I used mud and stone and brick and wood. Even the paint on the walls is non-acrylic; I used a plaster pigmented clay treatment on walls, and clay paint."

Stella's adobe is tiny, 900 square feet on an acre and a half of land. In such a space, the placement of every object is important; no object can be superfluous. Color and texture add richness without clutter, while an artistically arranged vignette, such as a crossed-base wooden console table with a selection of objects, a candelabra and a simply framed art print, becomes a focal point. Of course the outdoor space—in this case, a generous portal with rustic furniture, colorful textiles, a textural fence, carved columns and a bold blue door—almost doubles the living space. In a high-desert climate with 300 days of sunshine a year, that outdoor living space can be enjoyed even on warmer winter days.

Although Stella's personal spaces were in some ways worlds apart, they both had as their starting points simple, honest structures, each very much of its surroundings. "Both houses had a lot of potential," she says. "When a building speaks to me, as if asking for help to restore it to its true character, I find such invitations irresistible."

Surrounded by wisteria, cotton-wood, fruit trees and Russian sage, Stella's casita blends into the Santa Fe landscape.

FACING: Moroccan rugs, a bent-willow settee and rocks collected on camping trips furnish a quiet corner of the patio.

Bringing Modern into Traditional

ABOVE LEFT: A vibrant color scheme is offset by Santa Fe ristras, a vintage–style industrial light, French enameled house number plates and a cow skull from a friend's ranch in Mexico.

ABOVE RIGHT: A Rais wood–burning stove wards off Montana's chilly evenings, while gold walls and textiles in reds and oranges carry a unified palette throughout the house.

Stella furnished her living room with uphol–
stered pieces from Bombast in Vancouver and a
Noguchi coffee table. The side table is a petrified
rock from her family's ranch. She found the
Moroccan rug in the old medina in Marrakech.

FACING: An eclectic mix of dining chairs surrounds a 10-foot-long teak table brought from Stella's loft in Venice, California. The green antique trastero was purchased in Pasadena.

ABOVE: Noguchi paper light fixtures, an English pine hutch and oiled and waxed fir floors are in keeping with the simplicity of a quiet bedroom.

FACING: Patterned textiles and large Nelson pendant lamps complete the well–lit master bedroom.

ABOVE: Stella chose a light gray–green inspired by the Shaker palette for the wainscoting and painted the floor white. An antique cut–glass mirror enhances the natural light in the serene bathroom.

Intimate Pueblo

ABOVE LEFT: Al fresco living is a given in a sunny, high-desert climate. A dining table, Moroccan textiles, hand-carved columns, a Spanish colonial chest and a roomy settee stained black by Stella complete the outdoor "room." For doors and window trim, the designer chose a custom-mixed blue, traditionally believed to ward off evil.

ABOVE RIGHT: Wirehaired dachshunds Karma and Lulu await an outing.

LEFT: Stella composes compelling vignettes: a black vase by northern New Mexico artist Lisa Jensen, a Jack Spencer photograph and an antique New Mexican table purchased at Shiprock Gallery in Santa Fe. The figure sculpture, a prized possession, is by the designer's father, William Stella.

FACING: A photograph by Susan Stella hangs above a velvet–upholstered Eero Saarinen womb chair. The child's chair is eighteenth–century Guatemalan.

FACING: A homey, cheerful kitchen features blue tiles, classic red willow cabinet doors, a Mexican tin light fixture and a Ponderosa pine countertop over a whitewashed adobe brick base.

ABOVE: Native American beaded necklaces from Taos Pueblo and beyond.

LEFT: Turkish textured bed linens, a Donghia upholstered headboard, a Noguchi lamp and pots by Lisa Jensen stand out against the clay wall finish, whose rose earth color was chosen to reflect the hills surrounding the house.

FACING: A charming bath features Mexican Talavera tiles, a hand-painted mirrored wall cabinet and a 1930s New Mexican hand-carved chair.

For a Montana guesthouse adjacent to the year-round residents' modernist home, designer Abby Hetherington curated a collection of items that reflected the clients' hobbies and interests. An antler and fringe table by Cody, Wyoming, artisan Doug Nordberg is paired with a bench made from an old ore cart on wheels; the upholstery is a multi-colored woven leather fabric from Dedar.

Creative Spaces for Work & Play

Rustic outbuildings celebrate the relationship between indoors and outdoors in an unadulterated way while allowing the utmost play in expression. Barns, boathouses, guest cabins, tepees and other charismatic and idiosyncratic retreats are long on charm and redolent with atmosphere, whether they are working buildings like an equestrian complex or fanciful retreats, such as a wall tent perched high up in the foothills near Yellowstone and furnished entirely with vintage items.

Where primary living spaces are by necessity more about an ordered life, work and play spaces provide the perfect opportunity for creative expression and whimsicality. Bozeman, Montana, designer Abby Hetherington, who is known for her bold use of color, highly original ideas and sure sense of fun, proves this point in an outbuilding on a client's property just outside of town. The idea for the retreat, which is adjacent to but separate from the main house, is to serve as both a private space for houseguests and a funky clubhouse for the owners' teenage sons.

"We call it 'the Launch Pad,'" explains the owner, "because it's the perfect launch pad to Yellowstone Park, or for skiing, fishing or exploring."

In deference to houseguests, as well as to regional tradition, the structure, comprised of a living room with bar/kitchenette, guest room and bath, has that you-are-now-in-the-mountains vibe. But Hetherington put her original spin on the usual motifs. One wall is papered over in enlarged 1895 topographic maps of Park County (with hues changed to match the room's palette). The bedroom wallpaper is a trompe l'oeil design of stacked logs, and there's a bench made from an old ore cart. A working vintage neon BAR sign occupies pride of place above the hand-built bar.

"I wanted it to feel like a little 1970s hunting lodge," says Hetherington. "But I want every design to have a sense of humor. I want people to smile when they come in."

This doesn't mean the designer shuns typical rustic elements. She chose an Adirondack-style chair with a back made of skis for the entry, created a montage of fishing items with an elk mount on one wall, placed an antler side table next to the couch and sourced the rustic handmade bed from a local craftsman. But in making bold color choices and fusing traditional elements with the unexpected— an orange spray-painted coat rack, a bedroom lighting fixture dangling from a model of a hand, a bar top embedded with currency from all the family's travels—she creates festive spaces brimming with life.

"It may seem like mayhem," says Hetherington, "but it's what I call my 'bucket theory.' You want to be able to put everything in a bucket and shake it up and have it still work. This was a fun project because it really shows the owner's personality."

Work and play spaces provide the perfect opportunity for a homeowner's personality to shine. The place where one pursues one's passion is by definition a very personal, almost sacred, space. A wall tent built by musician/writer Dick Dillof is one such intimate spot. It is deliberately shared with few, precisely because it's a quiet retreat where he can ponder, write, and get away from the world. Perched up high in the Montana hills, with a spectacular view south into Paradise Valley and Yellowstone National Park, the canvas tent is furnished with items from another era: camp cots, vintage rockers, and an array of rare and vintage musical instruments Dillof collected over several decades.

"I had a similar canvas wall tent set up in the summers on an old mining claim in the Beartooth Mountains," he explains. "The tents are simple and impermanent, like tepees or sheepherders' wagons, both of which I've had before. Why did I put it up there on my hill? The obvious answer is to be up higher than my creekside home, where I'm able to sit and gaze out across the valley.

"I used to hike up there and sit on a big rock," he says, "but with the tent, I can spend hours up there protected from the elements. I can sit on the porch, or inside, feel the breeze blow through the tent, settle back in a bentwood rocker and play the banjo. There's a small stove on a table and I can cook, smoke a pipe and spend the night up there, with my instruments and things safe inside. A wood cabin is nice, and more protected from the elements, but canvas breathes and

lets in light and absorbs the smell of wood smoke and lets you feel more part of the land. I keep a spyglass up there and an old manual typewriter and a Victrola with some scratched-up 78s. What more do you need up there," he asks, "but maybe some good company?"

On the opposite end of the spectrum, work and play come together in a large-scale equestrian arena with a luxurious recreational space, commercial kitchen and private viewing quarters. Seattle designer LeeAnn Baker was tasked with creating comfort and refinement appropriate to the setting, while making sure the furnishings were durable enough to hold up to arena dust and cowboy boots. Nowhere was the design more carefully thought out than the areas necessary for the horses, such as wash stalls with concrete floors and rubber half-walls that give way to tile.

When the work is done, the horses put up and the dust washed off, tired equestrians can stroll over to an old ranch structure that has been repurposed as a gathering spot for family and friends. The slope-roofed calving shed, situated amidst mature cottonwoods near the Yellowstone River, is outfitted with a bar, a billiards table, comfortable couches, a wood-burning stove encased in a freestanding granite pillar, and a movie-viewing nook. Outside the weathered red walls, a fire pit draws stargazers and s'mores eaters.

"The entertainment space is a nod to the owner's father, for whom the ranch was home," explains Baker. Over the bar, a custom-made backlit stained glass sign advertises "Tighteners," a reference to what the prior ranch owner considered an essential end-of-day libation. In paying homage to her father, a daughter makes the ranch her own.

FACING: Writer–musician–troubadour Dick Dillof's wall tent retreat is a place of quiet and creativity. Outfitted with old camp items, vintage furnishings and fine–playing collectible instruments (which Dillof prefers for their sound), the wall tent is an ode to an earlier era. Bent willow rockers flanking an old rope-handled packing crate afford sweeping views south toward Yellowstone National Park. Says Dillof, "It's a place where I can spend the night, cook up some beans, play my instruments, keep dry and watch distant storms scuff up the sky."

ABOVE: Heart K Land and Cattle Company's state–of–the–art equestrian facility leads the way in marrying form and function for show jumpers and team ropers alike.

Launch Pad

ABOVE: The guesthouse living room references the immediate neighborhood through wallpaper custom made from an 1800s topographical map of Montana's Park County. Hetherington had it scanned, blown up and custom colored. The large round table on casters was designed by Hetherington and made by Misco Mill in Bozeman. It spins like a piano stool and can be raised and lowered—perfect for family dinners and the annual Super Bowl party. Hetherington had the red stool constructed from a butcher block top and a found metal base.

A vivid blue velvet sofa, colorful throw pillows, a vintage illuminated bar sign and a cabinet made from car parts by Jason Clary of Rusty Nail Design inject energy into the gathering space. The bar, made by the owner years ago and refurbished, has retro bar stools and a top embedded with currency from the family's travels.

Andrew Martin Lumberjack
wallpaper does much to
promote the cabin feel in the
bedroom, while interesting
objects found in the region and
gifts from family and friends
complete the quirky space.

Vintage Canvas

ABOVE LEFT: A wall tent overlooking hay meadows and the Yellowstone River can be opened on both ends to maximize breezes, the panoramic views and the night sky.

ABOVE RIGHT: Dillof composes on a folding war correspondent's typewriter of the sort used by Ernest Hemingway. He prefers the much-played fretless banjo for its bluesy, primitive sound. An 1890s concertina, which Dillof had restored, is perfectly suited to small spaces.

Though beautiful to look at, the instruments aren't for show. "They're my life's work, and their unique sounds create a mood and effect far different than recorded music." Though, Dillof admits, playing sentimental 78s, such as "Springtime in the Rockies," on his old Victrola can transport the listener to another time.

Durable Comfort

ABOVE: A meticulously designed and engineered horse complex—stalls, indoor arena, lounge, luxurious washrooms and private viewing area—has a sleek modernist–industrial vibe.

FACING: Wash stalls and public bathrooms are outfitted with elegant and durable fixtures and materials.

A living room/lounge with open
viewing into the indoor arena was
furnished for comfort and refinement
but designed to hold up under stable
dust and cowboy boots.

FACING: The Heart K rec room is a repurposed calving shed, highly appropriate on a working ranch. A high-efficiency wood stove takes the chill off even the coldest winter days.

ABOVE: The bar pays homage to the owner's father.

LEFT: A rustic fire pit makes the most of the weathered shed's riverside site.

On a New York farm, wood salvaged from the growing beds of mushroom barns provides a weathered contrast to a standing seam metal roof with snow guards and traditional glass globe lightning rods. The front hall leads to tall, west-facing windows with views of the Catskill Mountains.

American Farm Idyll

The irony of a perfectly sited and well-thought-out home is that what appears effortless is the result of wide-ranging references, patient observation and evolving vision. For New York designers Henry Smedley and Kathy Chow, the most crucial phase in building their home started well before the first hammer was lifted. It was the three summers spent camping on the property prior to beginning construction that most informed its design.

Each having grown up with a farm in their family background, the couple had hoped to re-create some expression of those experiences. They started with a map and drew a big circle outlining a two-hours' drive from Manhattan. Their only caveat was that they did not want to be able to hear traffic from their home. After crossing off beach areas and exploring along the Hudson River, they found their perfect paradise of rolling hills and big views in Dutchess County. "We were looking for a fixer-upper on a couple of acres," says Smedley, "and ended up with 40 acres and no house."

And then, most importantly, they paused.

During three years of getting to know the property, explains Smedley, "we learned how strong the winds are in the winter, where the best walks are and how to capitalize on the vistas. We learned how farmers think and how to keep the house and our other interventions on the property 'out of the way' and off productive farmland. This in turn allowed us to locate the entrance drive appropriately so it was not placed on farmable land. We had time to hear the stories from our neighbors about mistakes and opportunities they discovered in their time on their property. It also allowed time for us to learn about passive solar buildings and energy-efficient building means and methods. We were then able to challenge our architectural and building team to think a bit differently about that. It also allowed us time to 'soak in' the property and get to know it well. I weed-whacked paths through dense summer brush to learn about the topography of the land—where the steep parts were located and where the easiest places to walk were. As we cleared some paths, we realized from their tracks that the animals had figured all this out already!"

Ultimately, it was all about the land and its potential. "They say Montana is Big Sky Country," says Smedley, "but this really is big sky country too. It's 180 vertical feet from one end of the property to the other, and you can see the Catskills about 50 miles away. We're up on a hill and when looking around at the landscape the sky goes right down to the ground, for as far as you can see. Our large windows bring these views directly into the house."

Their property—half forested and half open fields, with rolling hills, some wetlands and a live creek on one end—offered ample opportunity for views, pastureland for cattle (they graze cow-calf pairs for a neighboring farmer), a vegetable garden, and quiet.

Smedley had studied architecture; both are professional designers. Both he and Chow knew they wanted a small house with a particular number of rooms. "We started with a fictional backstory that the house was a barn that had been messed with," explains Chow. "We also compiled a huge pinup board of inspirational reference photographs for the project." In searching for an architect, the couple loved JLF Architects' aesthetic and their masterful use of recycled materials. According to Paul Bertelli of JLF & Associates, "They loved the basics of what we're doing, and the values we brought to the regional context."

The process was extremely collaborative. Logan Leachman of JLF managed the architectural design process, while Smedley acted as on-site project manager, coordinating with Robert Bump Construction and working with subcontractors during construction. He has also built some of the furniture. After a weekend spent camping on the property, Smedley would roll out of his bed in the tent every Monday morning and attend the weekly construction meeting at 7:00 a.m.; by 10:00 am he'd be on his way to work in New York. Together the couple designed the majority of the interiors and sourced materials such as barnwood and salvaged items (old telephone insulators, doors, ventilation grates and a porthole that became part of a door, for example) from all over the Eastern Seaboard.

The house is built into the hill like an old New England barn. Says Bertelli, "People see the building and they love the way it sits in the landscape, the simplicity of the forms, and the scale of it."

And it is small, at about 2,700 square feet. The owners are proud of the fact that it was the smallest house their architect had ever designed and the smallest house their builder had ever built. The drive-through garage/woodshop is set at a right angle to the house; the result is a dooryard that has regional precedent. It's also a very functional space that becomes an extension of the house. With the doors of Smedley's woodshop opening into the dooryard, the frequently used south terrace, and the oft-visited pergola, much of the home's living space is actually outdoors.

With its smaller front windows, the house appears barnlike from the driveway. On the opposite side, says Smedley, "it's a more modern, a more cathedral-like space. It literally flows right to the outside." On the ground floor a compact powder room and streamlined kitchen open up to a large, airy great room with rustic materials, unique details and contemporary touches. Guest bedrooms are upstairs and the master bedroom is on the ground floor, while the laundry and mechanical equipment are housed on the lower ground floor, built into the hillside.

Although historic in form, the home is very modern in function. The siting and the windows were carefully conceived to maximize solar gain. A consultant was brought in to design the geothermal heating system, a series of four 280-foot wells that use underground temperatures to heat or cool the air. On wintry days, a cast-iron fire back sourced from a late-19th-century home in Chicago radiates heat. "That's what I love," says Smedley. "You have a new house with new technology, but it has a patina of old materials. You're not adapting to the way people lived 100 years ago. You have the best of the old and the best of the new too."

The safari-style tents and tepee are gone, but the original campsite remains, graced by a pergola for al fresco dining and by stone walls designed and built by the owners. "We didn't build where the original campsite was located, partly out of respect and partly to move up and see the distant valley," says architect Bertelli, "and it preserved the origins of the project."

For Smedley and Chow that was important. "Camping gave us an intimate understanding of our land: the seasons, the wind, day and night, and the rhythms of nature," Kathy Chow explains. "We gained a deep respect for dancing with nature . . . and she leads! This informed the siting, passive solar, and materials we used. And it created an enduring aura for our continuing art project."

Adds Smedley, "we also had the opportunity to figure out how comfortable the outside environment is most of the year on the land with nothing between us and outer space except for a thin layer of our atmosphere." "They also learned that electricity is not a necessity, for they always have lamp oil, a big fire and, once a month, a bright full moon.

A woodshed built by the owner and topped with a weathervane from a cousin's barn holds two winters' worth of wood. Patterned after Cuban tobacco barns, the floors are mesh, the eves vented. A pergola marks the owners' original campsite. Boulder walls terrace the steep slope.

In the main house, modern industrial windows are juxtaposed with a traditional bank barn structure. The large west-facing windows facilitate passive solar gain in cold weather, while geothermal cooling offsets summer heat.

RIGHT: The dining table was built from a fallen 250–year–old white oak from a family farm in Pennsylvania. The owners compiled hundreds of reference images for their project.

FACING: The large living room window is shielded by an over-hanging shed roof. The red industrial fan from Big Ass Fan Company was designed for use in barns. Owner Henry Smedley designed the Greek Revival bookcase.

LEFT: British encaustic tiles in the kitchen were inspired by cathedrals in Dublin.

FACING: Smedley and Chow got the idea for the insulators on the stair rails from lightning bugs; they light up. Pointed doors accommodate sloped ceilings. Small windows were found at a salvage company in Pennsylvania.

ABOVE: A guest bathroom takes its design cues from the 33rd Street subway station in New York City and Jules Verne's *20,000 Leagues Under the Sea*. The salvaged porthole is embedded in a custom sheet metal door.

FACING: The master bedroom features wood from a 100–year–old Amish barn, a salvaged door, and flooring from a 250–year–old white oak milled by the owners. The side table is an antique milk can.

In dramatic natural settings, designer Hilary Heminway feels that it's important not to compete with the view. She prefers simple, even spare fur-nishings. Antique keyhole chairs made by Thomas Molesworth and purchased through Fighting Bear Antiques retain their original red leather upholstery.

Grand (Under)Statement

Sometimes a grand statement is best made quietly. Whether a homesite has a built history or is relatively pristine, a thoughtful approach carried out at a deliberate pace yields dwellings that are site-appropriate, environmentally sensitive and modestly scaled—results that suit the needs of the occupants while honoring the land.

When a California couple bought property in Wyoming, their goal was to expose their young children to the kinds of idyllic outdoor moments they'd enjoyed growing up: fishing, star-gazing, lolling around on seemingly endless summer afternoons with a good book. "They wanted the experience of what Wyoming could give," explains designer Hilary Heminway. The result of their very patient process is "a one-broom house in a magical spot."

A wise landowner's first consideration should be the land: in this case a forested, wildlife-rich parcel blessed with a creek and wetlands. The property had been disturbed by past ranching and farming techniques; previous owners had built dams and berms to help control flooding. The original riparian edges had been lost, and wetlands and waterways had changed for fish and bird life. The new owner not only respected what was there, according to architect Paul Bertelli of JLF & Associates, but restored much of the pristine habitat.

One of couple's goals was to create a sense of sanctuary through modestly scaled buildings—a small cabin, a barn with guest accommodations, a teahouse for afternoon idylls—and a pond to attract coyotes, moose, elk and birds. "If you build a pond at a certain depth and length," explains Bertelli, "swans will occupy it in the winter. The homeowners built for that, and sure enough, they have a couple pairs wintering there."

The dwelling, a 900-square-foot cabin whose reclaimed wood and stacked stone exude timelessness, consists of two bedrooms and communal space with a lot of built-in cabinetry to make it work for a family and guests. "They don't mind packing everyone in," says Bertelli. "They're shooting for a sense of family and closeness, so they are doing everything together. There's no private library or TV room; it's more like, 'Okay, we're going to explore, or make a bonfire.' The communal aspects of the building foster togetherness."

The compact proportions of the cabin and the vast outdoor spaces combine to propel the family outdoors. A generous covered porch invites al fresco meals in all weather, but it's the teahouse, with its living roof and its dock jutting out over the pond, that provides a destination and sense of discovery.

Bertelli explains, "This family loves being outdoors and loves having a destination you have to walk to. The teahouse is built into the hillside, and is low down, at water level. With the green roof it looks like a bunch of rocks and meadow grass. It's just a screened porch with a deck out front with a pergola so you can sit in or outside. It's off the grid and has no power, but it does have a fireplace. They spend the summers there. They love having tents nearby. They'll build a little campsite and spend the night."

Bertelli credits his clients with patiently considering every potential before charting a course. The success of the project "is not mere serendipity," he says. "It has a lot to do with the amount of thought that goes into it."

For longtime Santa Fe residents Peter Buehner and Deborah Day, "thoughtful" would be the grandest understatement of all to describe their approach to a home that has fostered a lifelong appreciation of adobe vernacular and architecture. "It's taken us twenty years to get it 95 percent done," says Buehner. It's hard to visualize the home as they bought it in 1995. "It was derelict," Buehner says flatly. "The roof was leaking, the plaster was falling off the walls, several vigas were rotting and broken. The floors in the three original rooms consisted of three or four layers of linoleum over dirt."

The adobe's earliest three rooms dated back to 1885; later additions were added in the 1930s and '50s. The house sat on a bucolic acre, where the Buehners now tend chickens, guinea hens, an extensive vegetable garden and 29 fruit trees. It had water rights on a shared irrigation ditch originally built by Native Americans, a sheep pasture as an immediate neighbor and sweeping views of two mountain ranges.

When Buehner and Day bought the property, they knew it was going to need a lot of rehab. Buehner, a carpenter, was up to the challenge; he had decades of hands-on experience. Meanwhile, he and Day both volunteered with Cornerstones, a Santa Fe historic preservation group, where he learned invaluable skills in adobe repair and construction. Buehner had little previous experience with mud repair and brick laying before working with Cornerstones, but he was able to mix mud on the property, add sand and rebuild the walls. They re-plastered the inside walls of the entire house with mud, in some cases two to three inches thick because of erosion that had resulted from water running down the walls. They imported mud from a hillside on BLM land, mixed it with straw, mica and arroyo sand (which has a natural red tint), and plastered the whole house again in the mixture. "The walls are all natural, so anytime we need to fix anything we just spray it with a water bottle and add more mud. It's always good and the materials are always ready to go. Mud is a lovely material, a living material. It's the earth."

The 1880s portion still boasted its original Territorial trim, popular at the time. Buehner replicated it throughout the house, both inside and out. He remodeled the kitchen and bathrooms and built interior doors, cabinets, walk-in closets and the front door from scratch in his in-town workshop. "It took three years for us to move in, and another three years to finish the kitchen. We had a camp stove and a hot water spigot sticking out of the wall. I can't believe we did that," he laughs, "But I couldn't devote all my time to it because we were still working." At one point in the project, he recalls, they experienced a "catastrophic event" when a wall collapsed. "I was depressed for days," he admits.

In a manner particular to adobes, it seems rooted to its spot on the earth, appearing to grow from it. There is nothing jarring in its colors. It has no hard edges, no jumbled interiors. Rather, each room is a careful balance of volume and proportion. The uniquely tranquil color of the walls is not applied but imbued. The decor, a mixture of old and repurposed and new, has a Shaker-like serenity. Best of all, says Buehner, "when the sun comes into the living room and dining room from the French doors on the west side, it hits the walls or reflects off the floor and the wall sparkles because it has mica in it."

Two very different homes—one a halcyon family retreat from a fast-paced reality, one a primary residence for a couple fully integrated into their community—share a common approach: restraint in design. Likewise, they share a common success: structures that make grand statements as understated additions to the landscape they inhabit.

Peter Buehner and Deborah Day's Santa Fe living room decor takes its cue from the timeless solidity of adobe walls and timbered ceilings. Day sourced many of the blankets, pillows and rugs in the home from Guatemalan and Mexican sources and installed a Scandinavian wooden bench for fireside seating. Ornamental tin wall sconces were commissioned from local artisan and tin-art expert Maurice Dixon. The graceful chandelier with candles, a gift from a friend, was made by an El Paso craftsman.

Compact Cabin

ABOVE LEFT: Weathered wood and stacked stone lessen the visual impact of a home nestled into its environment among existing cottonwoods.

ABOVE RIGHT: A simple, compact kitchen makes the most of reclaimed materials. A rope and iron light fixture from Restoration Hardware hangs above counter stools chosen for their modern–retro vibe and their bounce.

FACING: A monolithic stone fireplace and simple wood mantel center the living room. Red Cowtan & Tout sofa fabric injects a jolt of color, while the large ottoman with antique kilim covering adds richness and texture. The burled lamp with hand-painted lampshade is an antique; metalwork artisan Bill Moore made the iron fireplace tools and screen.

ABOVE: Guest quarters over the garage feature a tiny coffee bar, antique bench, small dining table and floor-to-ceiling windows with simple curtains. The open sleeping area features a king bed and white bunks with Pendleton blankets.

ABOVE: The clutter-free master bedroom, with its iron bedstead and Native American rug, is a study in simplicity.

FACING: Weathered-wood bunk beds with Pendleton blankets and crisp white sheets, a modern standing lamp from Snake River Antiques, an African stool and a cheerful red chair furnish a children's room.

The Teahouse

A simple open–air teahouse on the edge of a quiet pond provides a family destination and is the perfect getaway for fishing, reading or napping. Al fresco meals on the deck define summer swimming parties, while a fire–place offers sanctuary on chilly days.

Living Serenity

ABOVE: White cabinets and trim create a crisp contrast against tinted adobe walls. The large cupboard, a Guatemalan antique, was purchased in Taos. The Godin cast-iron parlor stove from France has been owned by the couple for thirty years.

FACING: A bold zigzag-pattern rug and papier-mâché mask from Mexico stand out against otherwise spare interiors. The antique Mexican table is lit by an adjustable pendant on a pulley from the New York gallery Artemide.

ABOVE: A photo album chronicles the derelict state of the 1885 structure at the beginning of the project.

RIGHT: Deborah Day exercised restraint in her interiors; the approach creates serenity and shows the home's well-proportioned volumes to advantage.

FACING: A bedroom vignette features a textile by Scandinavian artist Pia Wallen folded atop an antique chest from Mexico.

Simplicity extends to the master bedroom, where a window bed adds seating and interest. The tumbled-brick floor extends through the French doors, offering a seamless transition from inside to out.

Rustic Revealed

Architect Larry Pearson loves the element of surprise. He enjoys creating built environments in which visitors engage through a process of discovery. Accordingly, for each new project, Pearson and his team think through every aspect of the approach, from the property's edge to the home's front door, then across the threshold and into the living space. He likes his homes to reveal themselves by degrees and will work to site access roads and outbuildings to this end. In the case of a home with a staggering view, this moment of revelation will make an even bigger impact.

Pearson Design Group was tasked with building a monumental log home on a steep, high-elevation site with far-reaching views. The clients desired that it be decidedly rustic yet still light and airy. The result is architecture that celebrates traditional form and vernacular but employs meticulous joinery, ultra-refined finishes, and spectacular amounts of glass. The home mixes chalet references with contemporary treatments, yet ultimately exudes a classic lodge feeling.

The entry to the home is elevated, with the approach an almost tunnel-like space created by a low, heavy-timbered shed roof and grounded by large boulders on the view side. Stepping across the threshold reveals the first surprise—a room with built-in benches and windows on three sides that yield a stunning panoramic alpine vista. (The concept was inspired by old-time sleeping porches.) From the entry hall one steps down into a long hallway then turns the corner to the great room. There the house begins to reveal its architectural drama in a much more vertical space, with soaring ceilings and elaborate timber truss work. A massive asymmetric stone fireplace provides a counterbalance to the glass expanses and anchors the house to the hillside.

The clients had been specific about their goals, but their goals didn't necessarily go hand-in-hand, Pearson relates. "The husband wanted logs and stone; the wife desired sophistication and airiness." Meshing their visions was a challenge everyone embraced.

Lead architect and project manager Josh Barr and the builders from Lowes Construction paid close attention to detail during the project in order to achieve a consistently refined aesthetic. Rustic materials such as logs and boards were rendered sleek and splinter-free, tightly scribed, smooth to the touch, and lustrous, the product of meticulously applied special finishes. The craftsmanship of the home is palpable; its effect is to elevate an otherwise rustic structure to an elegance found in far more refined interiors.

In the home's common rooms and bedrooms there's an emphasis on comfort and livability. The kitchen, with its bright surfaces, and the spa, with its Zen-like water feature, vaulted ceiling and heated tile lounge chairs offer opportunities for more contemporary influences. Of the light-filled kitchen (where generous windows are complemented by additional interior windows into an adjoining hallway to bring in light from the east), Pearson says, "It was so carefully orchestrated. We really tried hard to make it feel as though it could have been the shell of an old lodge that had been remodeled. Old lodges didn't have much glass; it was all about being protected from the elements. With the big walls of glass, it's almost as if you've remodeled it and opened it up to the world."

The one place that had no need for contemporary treatments was the guesthouse, a simple log cabin tucked into the trees. There, rustic reigns, from the vertical logs framing the door and powder room to the rugged stone fireplace, Molesworth-influenced applied-pole furniture, reproduction enamel appliances and birch bark ceilings. A door jamb made from a tree trunk, its roots extending into the room, signals the intention for a structure built not just as a private space for guests but as a retreat for the owners, the ideal hideaway for a late-night card game or profound meaning-of-life conversation.

In creating both worlds—the intimate den-like cabin and its counterpoint, a light-filled, view-dominant, timber-trussed main structure—the architects solved a very contemporary dilemma, perfectly bridging the gap between modernity and rusticity.

LEFT: The family room was designed for comfort and durability; fabrics are luxurious, and the copper drum table is both sturdy and beautiful. The large painting in the stairwell is by Theodore Waddell.

FACING: A ceramic antler chandelier from Roll and Hill serves as a focal point and creates a graceful contrast to the ruggedness of the stone fireplace. The chairs from Gregorius Pineo encourage lingering at the table.

FACING: Streamlined built-ins add storage without distracting the eye from the dramatic interplay of logs leading into the master bedroom area.

ABOVE: The kitchen was designed for clean lines and a feeling of light, achieved by white tiles, handmade in Montana, and white countertops. Tactile elements include horn drawer pulls, a zinc countertop and a hood detailed with hand-hewn beams and hand-carved corbels.

LEFT: A serene spa with vaulted ceiling features tiled heated loungers, a waterfall feature that runs along a trough under the floor and an ethereal chandelier from Porta Romana.

FACING: A corner fireplace in the master bedroom allows for a big window looking out at the dramatic mountain view.

Guesthouse

The guesthouse is a rustic hideaway, ideal for visitors as well as late-night card games. An applied-pole chair and ottoman by artisan Tim Groth work well in the wood-dominated interior. A simple wasp's nest is mounted above the fireplace, which is flanked by a series of mounted horseman artworks by Duke Beardsley. In the kitchen, birch bark ceilings and vintage-look appliances from Heartland complete the effect. A live-edge wood slab table floats above minimal metal legs and echoes the tree trunk doorway.

FACING: Minimal furnishings and vintage–like lighting fixtures allow the rustic elements to dominate.

ABOVE: A porch with a primitive chair and repurposed table keeps the focus on the great outdoors.

PUTNAM FADELESS DYES-TINTS

To Dye-Use Boiling Water   To Tint-Dip in Warm Water

EACH PACKAGE
DYES or TINTS
Wool. Silk. Cotton & Mixed Goods

USE PUTNAM NO-KOLOR BLEACH
TO REMOVE COLOR

MADE ONLY BY
MONROE CHEMICAL COMPANY QUINCY. ILL.

A guest apartment near Bozeman, Montana, was designed to feel like a bed-and-breakfast for houseguests. Designer Abby Hetherington and the home's owner turned their collecting for the project into a fun hobby that still continues today. Old Montana tins and other collectibles give the guesthouse the feel of a cabin in the woods.

New Rustic Tone, Texture & Whimsy

Three Montana homes, each fulfilling different functions—one is a primary residence, one a second home at a ski resort, the third a guesthouse for visitors to Big Sky Country—prove that a fresh approach to mountain rustic takes many forms. It need not be heavy and muscular, nor rely on a traditional palette or the usual visual clues. It can embrace color as way of injecting life and can boldly place more refined finishes against rustic elements. And it should feel free to repurpose, to layer, to mix and match patterns and styles and to find new ways of referencing standard western cultural mores.

The most traditional of the three, a classic Arts & Crafts bungalow with guest quarters over its combined barn and garage, embraces its inner nature and forays deep in the direction of cozy rustic. The tone is set at the entryway, where country collectibles telegraph a warm and cheerful welcome in an unabashed celebration of Americana. Upon entering, the multi-layered interior makes the most of its Craftsman-style trim and generously scaled fireplaces through comfortable furnishings and an extensive collection of visually interesting antique objets d'art. Through close collaboration between interior designer Abby Hetherington and her client (together they traveled on collecting trips east and to Europe), the assemblies are richly layered and masterfully arranged so that rooms appear lived-in without ever feeling cluttered or crowded.

The guesthouse, meanwhile, is a succession of charming vignettes, from the rustic display at the door to the vintage kitchen gadgets and containers, found items, repurposed lamps and "candy bar." Together the two modestly scaled spaces provide a supremely comfortable refuge during the long winters while offering generous porches for the clement seasons—the perfect balance for year-round mountain dwellers.

Freedom Lodge guesthouse is designed around a striking tower-like structure, a hallmark element of Pearson Design Group homes. At its summit, a square room with a hand-scribed log ceiling, central stone fireplace and windows on three sides comprises a veritable mountain aerie whose endless views cascade into the distance.

Rain Houser and Skye Anderson of PDG designed the interiors. Says Houser, "For this room, with its organic hearthstone and views straight out to the mountain ranges, the client wanted to make sure it was super comfortable and super durable. They wanted it livable." Furnished with couches whose primary mission is comfort; luxurious mohair-covered armchairs with leather arm covers; and a massive coffee table of rustic hewn beams floating above an invisible base, this is a room designed for parties, meals, après ski cocktails, working meetings—and, of course, naps.

Refined meets rustic in the bedrooms, where beds-as-sanctuaries incorporate upholstered headboards recessed into the wall to create cozy, private nooks for reading and relaxing. Omitting a headboard and bed frame saves space, while using luxurious fabrics and tufting the wall lends elegance, according to the designer.

Throughout the house, which was built by Lohss Construction—from the entry door with its hand-forged hardware and oversized rustic chair, to the internal log-framed doorway with "Freedom" spelled out in branch art above it—the house makes the most of its potential through bright ideas, well-placed art, and unique handmade touches.

Charlene Petersen of Cashmere Interior had never lived in the West before designing her own Rocky Mountain ski home in Montana. As a professional interior designer, she wanted to furnish her home in a site-appropriate manner yet avoid the clichés so common to mountain interiors. Her approach, she says, would be "a little more worldly, with a little African, a little Indian influence. But it's very important to me that a house looks like it belongs where it is."

Petersen achieved her own fresh rustic style by prioritizing clean lines, lightening traditionally masculine elements, and creating complex interiors using layers of patterns in harmonious tones. "In the first place, I wanted to make sure I kept everything very clean, with straight lines. Even if an upholstered piece is plaid, or a heavier-textured wool, it will have straight edges."

Mountain design, Petersen notes, typically has heavy iron or antler chandeliers; fixtures, then, provide opportunities to lighten the look. Large domes of clear glass illuminate the dining table, and in the living room, in a contemporary twist, open iron hoops reference traditional wagon wheel lighting. The strikingly beautiful fixture in the luxurious ski room is a clever play on the typical antler chandelier. In the stairwell, instead of a massive statement piece, a whimsical cluster of glass balls suspended from the ceiling shed ample light.

Petersen treats walls as opportunities to think outside the rustic box. Against the verve of some walls she maintains a balance of neutral spaces, using a gray wash for many surfaces and a natural finish on rough, reclaimed barnwood. The window trim, baseboards, and kitchen cabinets, for instance, are all in barnwood, which helps maintain a casual feel. The kitchen cabinetry employs modern flat-panel fronts to simplify the lines. Visual complexity, then, is all the more striking when it appears, such as in a powder room with cowhide tiles and in the kitchen with its bold Ikat-patterned backsplash. In a TV area she arranges baskets on a wall so that one can appreciate their arresting geometry. In a central open landing honored with three Andy Warhol paintings, a Navajo-inspired wallpaper injects a sense of fun, even quirkiness. In bedrooms she balances contrasting patterns on headboard, curtains and wall with neutral planes where the eye can rest. Combining a very large-scale pattern on the headboard, a medium-scale zigzag on the wall, and a small-scale pattern on the drapery creates harmony rather than chaos, Peterson says. "You don't want anything to fight for the limelight. If they're going to work together, they have to be a team."

In every room of the house, the vibe is warm and modern; comfort drives the selections and a healthy dose of whimsy sets guests at ease. In this home, as in the Craftsman bungalow and tower aerie, fun takes precedence over formality, and rustic meets refreshed.

For her own home, designed by Steve Gordon of Locati Architects, Charlene Petersen of Cashmere Interior juxtaposes vivid patterns against neutral backdrops. In the kitchen, Ralph Lauren fabric and pendants work well with wood expanses, while a bold backsplash of Ann Sacks tiles injects a liveliness into otherwise subdued hues. The stairwell is lit by a playful chandelier: a cluster of glass balls from Arteriors.

Cozy Arts & Crafts

ABOVE LEFT: A classic Arts & Crafts bungalow has a Greene & Greene–style door with jewel–colored stained glass. A concrete dog, old snowshoes and skis and other vintage items create the feeling of step–ping out of time.

ABOVE RIGHT: Hetherington and her client chose black velvet for Ralph Lauren chairs and a black back–ground on the paisley sofa fabric as a foundation to ground the room and complement the wood floors, beams and mantel. An English spaniel painting, hunting boots and the homeowner's silver collection keep the interiors from feeling too rustic.

ABOVE: A classic covered porch with antique pieces, found items, patriotic pillows and a deer mount create a comfortable outdoor living space.

RIGHT: An orange terracotta provides a welcome alternative to the light colors often chosen for the walls in compact spaces. It adds a richness to the room and is the perfect base on which to layer silver cups and a vintage Hermes tray.

FACING: A vintage Bull Durham poster, a lamp of found parts made by Misco Mill and a gaily painted chest of drawers compose a charming vignette.

Freedom Lodge

FACING: A stone and timber interior is softened with textiles and furnished simply with a round hall table, built-in bench and glass lighting fixture. The dramatic artwork, stone slab step and tree trunk newel post add visual interest.

ABOVE: In a living room with windows on three sides, furnishings are kept simple to avoid competing with the views. The table was designed by Rain Houser of Pearson Design Group and built by Integrity Builders. A painting by Duke Beardsley hangs over a rough-cut stone mantel.

ABOVE: A Duke Beardsley painting and wood-and-rawhide sconces illumi-nate a hallway leading to a guest bedroom.

FACING: The home's name spelled out in branches in the entrance hallway adds a classic rustic touch to refined interiors.

Plank walls were painted with a wash to achieve a homogenous tone while contrasting with the natural wood logs. In the bath, metal hardware and a sliding door inject a touch of rustic. In the bedroom, soft fabrics, muted tones and a tufted wool headboard set into an alcove foster a feeling of serenity. The metal silhouette of the pendants adds a feminine contrast to the headboard; a Moroccan rug adds visual texture and a soft landing.

Fresh Style

ABOVE: An extra-wide daybed furnished with throw pillows and sheepskins offers ample lounging in Charlene Petersen's great room. An egg chair from Restoration Hardware creates a sculptural statement against the bookcase surround, a hand-carved antique from India. The fireplace is constructed of Montana moss rock.

FACING: The zigzag motif found throughout the home is picked up in the massive cocktail table that anchors the great room.

FACING: Tall Schumacher–upholstered chairs surrounding a custom–made dining table create an intimate space within the larger room and are comfortable enough for long, leisurely meals. Oversized pendants from Urban Electric Factory cast a warm glow.

RIGHT: In the functional and elegant ski room, a generously proportioned ottoman in a Lee Jofa textile provides plenty of seating for removing boots. Red–framed closets add color, while the dark ceiling creates a back–drop that emphasizes the ethereal nature of the polished chrome antler chandelier from Roll & Hill.

LEFT: A bunkroom makes a fresh statement with its lively patterned textiles, large drum table and standing lamp with gently curved horn.

FACING: The diamond-patterned upholstered headboard stands out against a wallpaper inspired by arrows, a nod to Native American themes. An antique ottoman rests against the leather-covered bed.

Petersen chose to surprise guests on their visits to the powder room with a rustic sink of petrified wood set in an antique Chinese cabinet. A leather-detailed, brass-studded mirror is displayed against a dramatic raised-hair wallpaper from Elitis.

Acknowledgments

American Rustic is our third collaboration. It's been a lot of fun, but this book wouldn't exist without the talented design professionals whose work is included in these pages. So many of these gifted designers and architects are longtime friends as well as colleagues; each book project offers a chance to get to know them even better. And making new friends through these artistic expressions is one of the greatest benefits of the work.

The masters of the rustic genre have been incredibly generous with their time and talent: Paul, Logan, Becky, the designers and office staff at JLF Associates; Candace, Joe and all the gifted professionals at Miller Architects; Larry, Justin, Josh, Rain, Skye and their colleagues at Pearson Design Group. You are constantly pushing yourselves to collaborate with your clients in new and creative ways, and you set a standard to which others aspire.

Architect Clark Stevens and everyone at Carney Logan Burke—John, Eric, Andy, Darcey, et. al.—demonstrate what happens when environmental consciousness meets rustic architecture. Dan Turvey at Dan Joseph Architects and Todd and Rob at Highline Partners carried this to its fullest expression and in doing so set an example for others. Stephen Tobler's unique application of old-world techniques to modern-day realities is a revelation.

Interior designers Abby Hetherington, Susan Stella, Charlene Peterson, Laura Fedro, LeeAnn Baker, Erika Jennings at Carole Sisson and Elizabeth Dinkel shared their design expertise and opened their own homes and those of their clients. For their help and willingness to share their worlds, we thank Henry and Chow, Peter and Deborah, Frederick Howard, Jen Perry, Todd Thomson, Kirk Davenport and Carol Hudson. Thanks to Loneta Showell, Jami Supsic, Carter Walker and Seabring Davis for their friendship and support over the years. Terry Winchell of Fighting Bear Antiques has always been there for us with his invaluable perspective and encyclopedic knowledge of Native American and rustic art and artifacts.

Montana pals Dick Dillof, Ed, Mary and Jan at the Heart K and Tony and Lauren opened their Montana doors to us, while Stella, Pete and Deborah showed us Sante Fe hospitality. Hilary Heminway, Willy Matthews and Laura Barton's friendships have meant so much over the years, and their artistic influence has been inspirational!

As ever, this book would not exist without the expertise and dedication to quality typified by the team at Gibbs Smith, Publisher. Our heartfelt thanks to our editor Madge Baird, who responds to emails at all times of day and night with a gracious calm; to Gibbs Smith, our visionary; to Publisher and Creative Director Suzanne Taylor, for her enthusiasm for this project from the beginning; to book designer Sheryl Dickert and production designer Renee Bond, who make us look good. We are also so appreciative of Angela Gill, Lara Cilo, Kristen Newbern, Seonaid Campbell, Lucie Forstenzer and everyone else who helped us on the ground at each location during long days on the road.

Thanks to Audrey's support team: Todd and Scout, Coco and Larry, Patty and Aimee, Bill and Gail and all her Montana, Brazil and Kansas family. And to Collette, John and Emily for keeping her numbers straight. Chase couldn't get through the early morning writing sessions, ridiculously overscheduled road trips and round-the-clock editing without the backing of her family and friends. Deb and Dan, Audrey and Todd, Lisa and Alex, Sue and John, and Anne and Chris sheltered her, fed her and took her riding, hiking and fence-fixing on long scouting trips, while Dewey, Jimmy and Lynda provide technical expertise and the artisan perspective. Addie, Jessie, Ross, Katherine and Charles provide love, encouragement and much needed distraction on the home front.

We could not have done it without you!

—CRE & AH

Sources

Galleries

Fighting Bear Antiques
Jackson Hole, Wyoming
www.fightingbear.com

The Architect's Wife
Bozeman, Montana
www.architectswife.com

William Matthews Gallery
Denver, Colorado
www.williammatthewsstudio.com

Misco Mill Gallery
Bozeman, Montana
www.miscomill.com

Simpson Gallagher Gallery
Cody, Wyoming
www.simpsongallaghergallery.com

Urbaine Home
Bozeman, Montana
www.urbainehome.com

Visions West Gallery
Denver, Colorado;
Livingston & Bozeman, Montana
www.visionswestgallery.com

Designers

LeeAnn Baker
www.leeannbaker.com

Agnes Bourne
www.agnesbourne.com

Cashmere Interior
www.cashmereinterior.com

Elizabeth Dinkel
elizabethdinkeldesign.com

Laura Fedro Interiors
www.laurafedrointeriors.com

Hilary Heminway Interiors
hilary@hheminwayinteriors.com

Abby Hetherington Interiors
abbyhetheringtoninteriors.com

Carole Sisson Designs
www.sissondesigns.com

Stella
www.susanmstella.com

WRJ Design
www.wrjdesign.com

Architects

Carney Logan Burke Architects
www.clbarchitects.com

JFL Architects
www.jlfarchitects.com

Dan Joseph Architects
www.djawest.com

Locati Architects
www.locatiarchitects.com

Miller Architects
www.ctmarchitects.com

Pearson Design Group
www.pearsondesigngroup.com

**Clark Stevens,
New West Land Company**
www.clarkstevens.com

Stephen Tobler
www.stephentobler.com

About the Author

Chase Reynolds Ewald has been writing about food, design, travel and lifestyle in the West and beyond for 25 years. A graduate of Yale and the Graduate School of Journalism at U.C. Berkeley, she is currently Senior Editor of *Western Art & Architecture Magazine*. This is her eighth book and her third collaboraton with Audrey Hall.

About the Photographer

Audrey Hall's images about culture, style and travel are diversely featured, from social media campaigns to television. She was recently on the road in Africa, Haiti and domestically with Pulitzer Prize–winning journalist Nicholas Kristof for the PBS series *A Path Appears*. This is her tenth book.